Demetrius

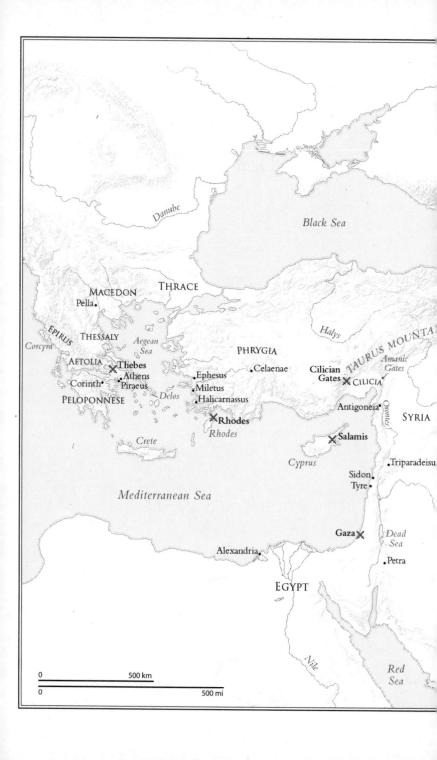

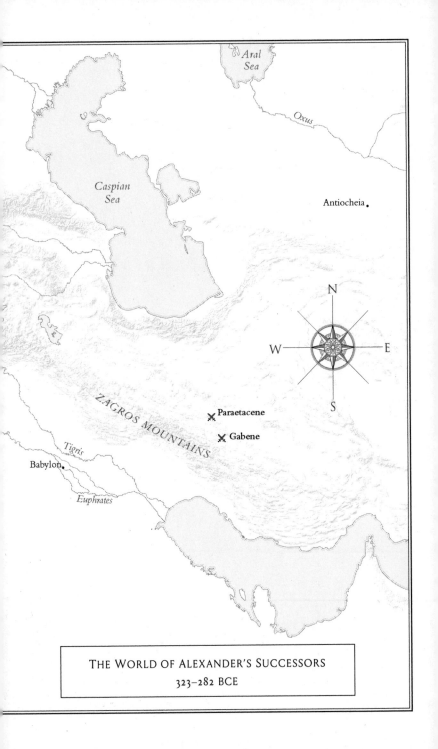

Aral
Sea

Oxus

Caspian
Sea

Antiocheia .

N

W   E

S

ZAGROS MOUNTAINS

Paraetacene

Gabene

Tigris

Babylon .

Euphrates

THE WORLD OF ALEXANDER'S SUCCESSORS
323–282 BCE

Demetrius

Sacker of Cities

James Romm

· ANCIENT LIVES ·

Yale
UNIVERSITY PRESS
NEW HAVEN & LONDON

Published with assistance from the foundation established in memory of
Amasa Stone Mather of the Class of 1907, Yale College.

Yale University Press books may be purchased in quantity for
educational, business, or promotional use. For information, please e-mail
sales.press@yale.edu (U.S. office) or sales@yaleup.co.uk (U.K. office).

Set in the Yale typeface designed by Matthew Carter, and Louize, designed by
Matthieu Cortat, by Integrated Publishing Solutions, Grand Rapids, Michigan.
Printed in Great Britain by TJ Books Ltd, Padstow, Cornwall.

Frontispiece: Beehive Mapping.

Library of Congress Control Number: 2022931846
ISBN 978-0-300-25907-0 (hardcover : alk. paper)

A catalogue record for this book is available from the British Library.

10 9 8 7 6 5 4 3 2 1

· ANCIENT LIVES ·

Ancient Lives unfolds the stories of thinkers, writers, kings, queens, conquerors, and politicians from all parts of the ancient world. Readers will come to know these figures in fully human dimensions, complete with foibles and flaws, and will see that the issues they faced—political conflicts, constraints based in gender or race, tensions between the private and public self—have changed very little over the course of millennia.

James Romm
Series Editor

Contents

Contents

Demetrius

CHAPTER ONE

His Father's Son

On a long winter night in 322 BCE, a one-eyed man and his teenage son made their way to the coast of what is now Turkey, traveling west from a point far inland. Probably they followed the river Meander, whose winding course has given the English language a word for slow wandering. But their movements were anything but slow or indirect. They hastened toward a fleet of Athenian vessels, a convoy waiting for them at a rendezvous point. Boarding those ships under cover of dark, they set sail for Greece — in secret, for their journey was made in defiance of standing orders, an act of insurrection against the ruling regime.

The man was Antigonus One-Eye, otherwise known as Cyclops, so named for his mangled face. He had lost an eye in his younger days, hit by artillery fire while fighting under King Philip of Macedon. A metal bolt from a crossbow-like weapon had lodged in his eye socket, but the big, bearish man had refused to withdraw or seek medical aid until after the battle was won. His son was Demetrius, by now nearly as tall as his father, but very different in looks: unscarred, smooth cheeked, and extraordinarily handsome —

so much so that later in life he was followed around in the streets by gawking admirers trying to get a good look.

The lands through which the pair traveled were astir with unease and confusion. Alexander the Great had died some months earlier in Babylon, quite suddenly and without a viable heir. The empire he had ruled, stretching from modern Albania to eastern Pakistan and south to Egypt — two million square miles in extent — was up for grabs, and numerous hands seemed to ready to grab it. His empty throne had supposedly been filled, but by *two* kings, his son and his half-brother — the former an infant born after his death, the latter a man in his thirties but, due to a disability, mentally unsound. Neither could exercise power of any kind, certainly not the iron-fisted control needed to hold such a vast realm together. Four regents were governing on their behalf, in a complex arrangement that seemed likely to produce discord and invite defiance.

Indeed, it was defiance that had sent Antigonus and his son westward, across the Aegean toward Greece. The chief of the four-man board, a general named Perdiccas, had ordered Antigonus to move *east* with a contingent of troops to support one of *his* close allies — a servile task and an affront to dignity. Antigonus had ignored the order, and Perdiccas, incensed, demanded that he stand trial. His demand, along with a piece of alarming news Antigonus had received, had prompted the hasty departure. Perdiccas, it had been learned, though officially just a caretaker for the two kings, was planning to marry Alexander's sister Cleopatra — a move that suggested a bid for the throne on his own part.

The time had not yet come when kings could be created ex nihilo from outside the Argead family, the dynasty that had ruled Macedon from its earliest days. Strangely enough it would be Antigonus himself and his son Demetrius who would assert this prerogative, becoming, in modern terms, Antigonus I and Demetrius

I, crowned heads of state — though of *what* state, no one was certain. But that day was as yet more than fifteen years off, after many a battle had been fought, many leaders had fallen, and the empire had fractured and split, with war zones at all of its seams. Amid that carnage, Demetrius would rise high on a surge of humanity's hopes. He would seem like — or would try to become — a new Alexander, restoring wholeness and peace to a broken world.

Perhaps Antigonus had already glimpsed that his fortunes might rest on the tall, athletic boy with exquisite features. Why else did he take his son along on this dangerous journey? His own generation, men in their sixties with bushy beards and battle-scarred faces, was quickly losing ground in the world Alexander had built. Those who now held the reins of the empire, the Babylon clan, were in their forties or even their thirties, clean-shaven after the fashion of Alexander. Smooth cheeks, flowing hair, and a melting, faraway gaze — that was how Alexander was always depicted, a portrait he had carefully curated during his life. Even in death, that image held people in thrall. All who sought power over the next centuries would try to conform to the template.

Or perhaps Antigonus meant this midwinter voyage on storm-tossed seas to be an apprenticeship for his son, a lesson in autonomy and pride. If the family had been slighted — as clearly it was by the orders Perdiccas issued — then the family must seek out those who would give it respect. In Europe were men of Antigonus's stamp who shared his mistrust of Perdiccas and the Babylon regime. Chief among these were Antipater, by now nearly eighty years old, guardian of the Macedonian homeland and its Greek vassal states, and Craterus, formerly one of Alexander's officers, now working hand in glove with Antipater and married to his eldest daughter, Phila. With these two as allies, Antigonus and his son need not bow before Perdiccas or stand for his rumored marital power play.

So father and son climbed aboard an Athenian ship, accompanied by a few loyal friends and by soldiers. Their trans-Aegean voyage is the first event recorded in the life of Demetrius — a fitting start to his tempestuous career. Over the next four decades, he would cross those seas many times, as the fates drove him from coast to coast and from continent to continent, tossing him down on one shore only to lift him up on another. He would never have peace, nor allow any others to have it, as the crazy zigzags of his life brought turmoil to much of the globe.

The wars of the Successors — the men who sought to control Alexander's empire — had begun.

Perhaps the teenaged Demetrius still remembered Macedon, the land of his birth, for he spent the first years of his life there in the mid-330s. Those were years of huge change in his homeland. King Philip, father of Alexander, had transformed a small regional power into the lord of all Greece, defeating the two reigning states, Athens and Thebes, and setting up forts and garrisons to smother dissent. With an army he had equipped and trained in new tactics, with siege machines his engineers had invented, Philip had seemed capable of defeating any foe, even the Persian Empire, a massive but aging world state. Indeed he was planning an invasion of that realm when, in 336, an assassin cut him down. Alexander then came to the throne, a young man of twenty, and carried through his father's plan to conquer the East.

The Greeks went along on Alexander's anabasis, his march into Asia, some willingly, others less so. Unaccustomed to domination by kings, the Greeks still resented Macedon's supremacy, but Alexander showed that he would use force to keep them in line. Some seven thousand Greek soldiers accompanied the Macedonian army, officially classed as allies but essentially hostages. They made little difference to Alexander's combat strength, since they fought with seven-foot spears rather than the huge new *sarisas* developed by Macedon — fearsome pikes more than twice that length. But their presence there, under watchful Macedonian eyes, ensured the good behavior of their home cities in Greece.

Antigonus, Demetrius's father, had been put in charge of this Greek contingent, an important but inglorious assignment. He crossed into Asia with Alexander's army in 334, leaving behind his son and his wife, Stratonice. No doubt he planned to fight in the front lines and advance to bigger and better commands, but Alexander had other ideas. Perhaps mistrusting men of advancing years, Alexander slotted Antigonus into a rear-guard post: mopping up pockets of Persian resistance in western Anatolia. The province called Phrygia, today part of Turkey, became his domain, and the palace in its capital, Celaenae, his home. At some point after pacifying the region, he sent for his family to join him at his new seat.

In the next ten years, as others won glory and riches, Antigonus lived the life of a regional governor, an administrator, not a conquistador. He took no part in the cavalry charges, the breakneck pursuits, the exploration of far-off Indian lands — all the adventures that made Alexander a legend and hardened his troops into fearsome killing machines. Amid the pleasures of hunting and feasting, he raised his two sons: Demetrius had been joined at some point by a younger brother, Philip. This might have been a good enough life for a Macedonian baron, but then came Alexander's death, and everything changed.

A decade in Phrygia had put Antigonus outside the circle that now had control of events. Alexander's closest friends and lieutenants — Ptolemy, Perdiccas, Lysimachus, Eumenes — had fought and traveled together throughout that decade; to them, Antigonus was a virtual stranger, still more so Demetrius, whom they had met only as an infant, if at all. Perdiccas in particular hated Antigonus for reasons that are unclear, and spread false reports designed to blacken his name. Perhaps these included the rumor preserved by Plutarch that Demetrius was not really Antigonus's son but his *nephew*. Any parents who are proud of a child they have raised can imagine how *that* must have felt.

Antigonus found a natural ally in Antipater, who had also been left behind and left out of the eastern conquests, and in Craterus, who had been sent home from the front despite his stalwart service. Antipater had never crossed into Asia at all but had loyally guarded the homeland in Alexander's absence, subduing Greek challenges to Macedonian rule. Of late he had found himself in tough straits, besieged and nearly starved into surrender by rebellious Athenians, but Craterus had come to his rescue. By now these two were firm partners, their bond cemented when Craterus married Phila. Together these kinsmen were pursuing a tough campaign in Aetolia, putting down more Greek defiance, when Antigonus and Demetrius arrived, fresh from their midwinter voyage.

The Aetolians were in a bad spot. Antipater had them trapped in snowy mountain redoubts, cut off from food supplies; they could not hold out much longer. But the arrival of Antigonus and his son proved their salvation. When these two conveyed news of Perdiccas's marital plans and described how callously they themselves had been treated, Craterus and Antipater were appalled. The idea that Perdiccas might overmaster them all seemed much more urgent a crisis than a ragged band of Greek rebels. They dropped their blockade and forged a quick truce with the Aetolians. Then they made their troops ready to march. Craterus, it was decided, would take an army to Asia and bring Perdiccas to heel. Antigonus would return to the Anatolian coast and support that attack.

By the terms of a settlement crafted just after Alexander's death, Antipater and Craterus shared control of the empire, but they were meant to remain in its European quadrant. The lion's share of the land and wealth lay in Asia, under control of Perdiccas. This split, though uneven, might have satisfied all, had not the one-eyed man and his son crossed the sea and raised the alarm. Now all bets were off; the contest for empire no longer had any boundary lines. Craterus made ready to fight the forces of Perdiccas, even though it meant fighting his own countrymen.

Craterus would leave behind him his newly wed bride, Phila, now in her late thirties and renowned as one of the leading women of her time. In childhood she had been her father's wisest adviser; as a young woman her virtues were said to outshine even her beauty. She was married first to a man named Balacrus, who was killed in battle, and by him had a son named Nicanor; to her second husband, Craterus, she had also borne a son, named after his father. A third marriage awaited her, as we will see, that would test her moral and emotional strength.

Their mission accomplished, Antigonus and Demetrius returned to their ships, now leading an army of three thousand. They retraced their route back to Asia, to set about winning, or forcing, the allegiance of its western provinces. Once Craterus crossed into Asia, they knew, the die would be cast and the cities of Anatolia would need to choose sides. It was their job to make certain those cities made the right choice.

In just a few months, the life that Demetrius knew in Celaenae — a pleasant amalgam of riding, hunting, and feasting — had been utterly shattered. Though he could not yet know it, such a life was now wholly a thing of the past. A future of battles, sieges, invasions, and conquests awaited the boy and his father until the end of their days.

——

The empire of Alexander had become an enormous game board with multiple players. The contestants' main objective, thus far, was to control the two kings, Alexander's toddler son and mentally damaged half-brother, the only male heirs left in the royal family. Though neither heir could act on his own behalf, the names and the seals of these two stood atop official decrees; their authority opened the treasuries of Asia, huge caches of gold and silver in fortresses and holdfasts. For the moment, these hapless monarchs resided with Perdiccas, and this gave him the right to act as surrogate king.

This game had no rules, for it had never been played. The Macedonians had never commanded a global empire, nor had their army been scattered across three continents, until a few years before Alexander's death. Decisions once taken around the king's banquet table, in a seat of government recognized by all, now had to be made by slow exchanges of heralds among widely diffused armed camps — if they could be made at all. Mistrust among Alexander's lieutenants grew and festered, augmented by distance. By private envoys they sought to form leagues with those they deemed useful or plot against others who seemed to stand in their way.

As they crossed back to Asia in 321, Antigonus and Demetrius were about to enter this game, soon to establish themselves as its leading contestants. But another player was also declaring himself at this same time, a man with whom they would vie for the next two decades. Ptolemy, son of Lagus, a friend and companion of Alexander's since boyhood, had gotten control of Egypt, the empire's richest and most defensible province. In a daring roadside heist he had hijacked Alexander's funeral hearse and brought the king's body to Memphis, his capital city, a talisman supporting his claim to be Alexander's true heir.

Ptolemy's theft of the corpse and the rebellion it implied came at a lucky moment for Antigonus and his son. Their ally Craterus was coming across the straits to invade from the north, and now Perdiccas had to confront a southern challenge as well. It was he from whom the corpse had been stolen, and such an outrage could not be left unanswered. Fighting on two fronts, Perdiccas had to divide his forces; he gave some to his righthand man, Eumenes, to stop the advance of Craterus through Anatolia, and took others with him to ford the Nile and attack the renegade Ptolemy. He sent a third contingent to Cyprus to secure a naval base supporting the Egypt campaign. Antigonus and Demetrius, therefore, their mission in Anatolia largely successful, led their own small army to Cyprus to counter this operation.

Demetrius was now of an age when a modern youth might head to college, but he was getting a different kind of schooling. The world was suddenly wider, and movement of forces more fluid, than ever before. Reports arriving in his Cyprus camp tracked events on three continents at once; fleets, land armies, even herds of elephants were in motion, synchronizing their movements with those of allied forces, preparing for clashes with foes. Demetrius watched his father orchestrate these movements in league with Craterus and, in Europe, Antipater. He had begun his apprenticeship in global war, the trade he would pursue throughout much of his life.

There was every reason to think that Craterus would defeat Eumenes, who was not even Macedonian by birth. Craterus had only to remove his helmet and show his face, he believed, and Eumenes' troops would desert to his side, choosing a Macedonian compatriot over an interloper. But Eumenes had recruited and trained a cavalry corps from the peoples of Anatolia, foreigners who neither knew nor cared who Craterus was. They charged him and caught him off guard, unhorsing him and trampling him under their horses' pounding hooves. In the first of many strange twists in the wars of the Successors, a man respected by all as a natural leader, one of Alexander's top officers, fell prey to an upstart Greek.

Meanwhile, in Egypt, Perdiccas was having trouble getting across the Nile. He tried to ford it alongside his elephants, hoping the massive beasts would break the force of the current, but this was a fatal mistake: their heavy tread stirred up the streambed and suddenly deepened the channel. Two thousand men, fully a third of his forces, were caught in mid-crossing and swept away by the flow, many into the jaws of waiting crocodiles. The survivors could not bear the agony of this loss, caused seemingly by their commander's ineptitude. A group of conspirators led by an officer named Seleucus stabbed Perdiccas to death in his tent. New guardians were put in charge of the kings (for the two monarchs had accompanied the expedition), and the army made its way back to Asia. Other generals hastened to rendezvous with it, including Antigonus One-Eye and his handsome son.

Arriving from Cyprus at Triparadeisus, a hunting resort in what is now Lebanon, Demetrius found himself at a conclave of global importance. Antipater had arrived from Europe, his first trip overseas, to try to take charge of events. The two kings were there: Alexander IV, now two years old, attended by his mother, Rhoxane, daughter of a Bactrian tribal chief, and Philip III with his new bride, an Illyrian teenager. Soldiers were everywhere, some brought from Europe by Antipater, others serving under Antigonus, a third contingent—dangerous men—the army that had invaded Egypt and killed their commander, Perdiccas. Among this last group was

Seleucus, who had shown by his leadership of the assassination plot that he had a large role to play in the contest ahead—though no one could yet guess *how* large. Somehow these disparate factions had to form an assembly and find a way forward.

The problems facing the empire were starkly revealed at this meeting. The Perdiccan army, tough veterans of Alexander's wars, were accustomed to getting sackloads of loot, but the Egypt campaign had not paid off. They started raising a row over pay they felt they were owed. When Antipater entered their camp to calm things down, they seized him and might have torn him apart, had not Antigonus One-Eye charged into the fray to rescue his senior ally. Both money and trust were clearly in short supply, and the troops had shown how little respect they had for *any* commander, now that the man they adored as a god—Alexander—was a corpse, and a purloined one at that.

But a common enemy could still bring these factions together, and they found one in Eumenes, who had orchestrated the death of Craterus. As an officer of the fallen Perdiccas, Eumenes was easily demonized, especially since, as a Greek, he was seen as a foreigner. The conclave at Triparadeisus declared Eumenes an outlaw and resolved that he must be destroyed. Antigonus One-Eye asked for, and received, the task of destroying him. To that end he took control of the army that had marched on Egypt and, more important, custodianship of the kings.

In an instant Demetrius saw his family's fortunes soar. The sovereignty of western Asia, and perhaps a good deal more, had been laid at the feet of his father. The opportunities must have seemed boundless. Perdiccas and Craterus were dead, Ptolemy seemed content (for the moment) to remain in Egypt, Antipater, in his late seventies, was too old to mastermind wars that spanned continents. It was up to Antigonus to control the empire's center of gravity, western Asia. And as Demetrius knew, whatever his father controlled might very well someday be *his*.

But before any steps toward this illustrious future were taken, before the crusade against Eumenes could be launched — an effort that would consume much of the next five years — Demetrius was given a very different assignment. Unexpectedly, and entirely against his own will, he was about to get married.

Like most adolescents, Demetrius was interested in sex, indeed more interested than most, in part because his good looks and family wealth gave him more opportunities. By the time of the Triparadeisus conclave he had already gained a reputation for philandering. In his family's palace at Celaenae, young women had come and gone from his bed in a manner that caused his father to wink at him knowingly with his one good eye. One day when Demetrius ignored his father's summons, claiming he had a fever, Antigonus went to the boy's chambers and spotted a hetaera, a courtesan, furtively slipping away. As he entered his son's room, Demetrius stuck to his story: "The fever has left me," he declared. "Yes, I met it just now as it went out the door," his father replied.

A sober, serious woman more than twice his age, twice widowed and with children from both unions, was certainly not the bride Demetrius would have sought, had he even wanted to wed. But Phila, the widow of Craterus, was now a free agent and a worthy dynastic prize. As a woman of known moral virtue, she conferred dignity on any man she might marry, and she carried with her as dowry the favor of Antipater. Since this great lord controlled eastern Europe, a marital alliance between him and the house of Antigonus, who had just become lord of western Asia, was very much in the interest of both parties and, indeed, the whole empire.

Such a union might cement the bond of the continents established by Alexander but already fraying—especially if that union produced a male child.

Given what was to be gained, the age gap between bride and groom was of little importance, still less the vast gulf between their temperaments. Nonetheless, Demetrius made his displeasure known to his father. In reply Antigonus whispered a verse of Euripides in his son's ear, cleverly changing a single word while keeping the meter intact. In the play *Phoenician Women,* the son of Oedipus, Polynices, describes how he lay in wait, keeping silent in servile fashion, as he looked for a chance to seize power in Thebes: "One must be a slave, if it leads one to profit." Antigonus wittily rephrased the line: "One must be a *groom,* if it leads one to profit." Presumably his son knew Greek drama well enough to appreciate the joke.

Perhaps what pained Demetrius even more than Phila's age and gravity, was the thought that she would be his *only* wife. Polygamy was permitted to Macedonian *kings*—Alexander the Great had taken three wives, his father perhaps seven—but not, thus far, to men outside the royal line. The thought of a lifelong bond with one woman, albeit not an exclusive one (given the license granted to high-ranking males), must not have appealed to a randy, adventurous youth. Little could Demetrius guess that this bond would one day, decades hence, redeem him from political ruin and win him a throne.

The details of the wedding are unknown. Presumably Phila was brought to Triparadeisus from Macedon, where she had thus far remained, for the nuptial rites. She soon became pregnant and bore her third son, who received his grandfather's name, Antigonus. To distinguish him from One-Eye, he came to be known as

Antigonus Gonatas, perhaps "Antigonus Knock-Knees" (but the meaning of the epithet is obscure).

Demetrius was growing up fast. At the age of eighteen, he had become a husband and a father. It remained for him, in accord with the patrilineal patterns of his day, to become a leader of troops.

CHAPTER TWO

The Apprenticeship of a General

The conclave at Triparadeisus broke up and the hunt for Eumenes commenced. Antipater and Antigonus, their alliance cemented by the marriage of their eldest children, took separate armies and headed north. Eumenes was marauding through Asia Minor at the head of an Anatolian cavalry, horsemen who knew no allegiance to Macedon, only to their new Greek paymaster. He was proving a clever opponent. Rather than engage in a head-on fight, Eumenes played hit and run, living off the land and amassing plunder by sacking small towns and estates. At one point he audaciously occupied Celaenae, Antigonus's capital, while the one-eyed man and his troops were elsewhere. Though he no doubt relinquished that city as soon as his foe reappeared, the insult must have stung.

Yet it seems that Antigonus bore no malice toward Eumenes, a man he had known only briefly more than ten years earlier. His reason for chasing this Greek was purely political: Alexander's veterans considered Eumenes a traitor, and it was on the backs of these troops, the "royal army" as they are sometimes known, that the fate of the empire rested. Their reputation for battlefield prowess and their long experience under Alexander made them seem super-human — as they were very much aware. They had already made it known at Triparadeisus that their demands for pay or for power could be ignored only at their commanders' peril.

The chase went on, month after month, with Eumenes always staying just out of reach. Meanwhile, Antigonus lost one of his most precious assets, the trust of Antipater. It was by Antipater's nod that he had gained command of the kings, but the old man had had his misgivings; One-Eye's imperious style seemed disturbing, perhaps a sign that he, like Perdiccas, had royal ambitions. After hearing reports to this effect from his son Cassander, Antipater asked that the kings be surrendered to *him* and brought back to Europe. He took charge of the hapless monarchs and with them crossed the Straits of Hellespont (the modern Dardanelles), returning to Macedon. He left his troops with Antigonus to carry on the war against Eumenes.

Demetrius observed these maneuvers, perhaps from a distance; it is not clear whether he marched with his father or stayed at home in Celaenae with his new bride. He was glimpsing the mutual jealousies of the great leaders, which demanded that any surge forward by one be quickly pulled back by the others. If no single commander could rule, each might at least ensure that none of the others outstripped him. A balance of power was always maintained. This principle was to be crucial in what lay ahead for the youth.

Antigonus chased Eumenes through much of Asia. With feints, dodges, and tricks, the two generals tried to outsmart each other, "fighting on the front lines of intelligence" as the chronicler Diodorus puts it. Antigonus came to respect his adversary's talents: after trapping Eumenes in a mountain fortress and putting him under siege, he offered to call off hostilities and join forces instead — a re-markable case of pragmatism outweighing nationalism. Eumenes seemed to agree to the deal and was freed, but then slipped out of the pact by way of a verbal loophole. The duel resumed, with Eumenes falling back eastward toward what is now Iran.

By this time Demetrius was certainly marching in his father's retinue, through the tough Zagros Mountains, a route forced on them when Eumenes blocked other paths. Plutarch has preserved one anecdote that probably comes from this march, an uncharacteristically tense exchange between father and son. Demetrius asked in an evening planning session what time the army should break camp the following morning. His father snapped back, "Are you worried that you alone won't hear the trumpet sound?" The one-eyed commander was wearied by several years in the field and impatient to catch his quarry before winter set in. Even his beloved elder son might try his patience.

By tricks and deceptions, Antigonus finally forced Eumenes to stand and engage on two different battlefields within two months' time. Antigonus had by this time amassed an army of 28,000 infantry and 8,500 cavalry, plus 65 war elephants, part of the herd that Alexander the Great had brought back from India. Eumenes too had a sizable force, including the 3,000-man unit known as the Silver Shields — an elite infantry corps that had served with such distinction in the East that Alexander had coated their weapons with silver. Now in their sixties and even seventies, these men had been honed to a razor's edge by long years of service and were widely regarded as invincible. It was they, in the end, who were to decide the outcome of the years-long duel between Antigonus and Eumenes.

Demetrius, now nineteen, was assigned a lead role in both battles: command of a cavalry corps on the crucial right wing. This was an impressive post for a youth who had never before seen combat. Antigonus knew he was putting his son in harm's way, but he had an illustrious model. At Chaeronea, some two decades earlier, in a fight against Athens and Thebes, King Philip had given his son Alexander, then eighteen years old and also fighting his first major battle, a crucial role and position. Leading the *left* wing that time, where he faced the storied Theban Sacred Band, Alexander was tasked with striking the killing blow. His victorious charge at Chaeronea had laid the foundation of his legend, binding the soldiery to him in loyalty.

Antigonus followed this script when he brought his son forward to fight Eumenes. If Demetrius could reenact the valor of Alexander, he would gain the respect of the troops — tough, ornery men whom no one, not even Antigonus, had thus far entirely controlled. A handsome youth on a charging steed might capture their imagination, as Alexander had done, and win their allegiance. To further these parallels, Antigonus had given a resonant name to the cavalry corps that Demetrius would lead: the Companions. As everyone knew, this name had belonged to Alexander's elite horsemen, the unit he headed throughout his Asian campaign.

Antigonus took steps to protect his son's life and handsome visage in both battles. He stationed himself on Demetrius's right, at the head of another cavalry corps, the light-armed, swift-moving Tarentines. These expert riders, named for the town in southern Italy where their style of fighting was forged, could be dispatched at speed to assist Demetrius should he get into trouble. Antigonus clearly meant to apprentice his son in generalship, but without too much risk, and, if possible, allow him to strike the decisive blow. For that had been the task of the Companions as Alexander designed them: in the wedge-shaped formation called an *embolon* they drove into enemy lines like the ramming prow of a warship and broke apart all but the tightest formations.

We would like to have a description from either of these two battles of how Demetrius charged at the head of this wedge, for that seems to have been how both the clashes began. But our sources keep their eyes on Antigonus instead. It was he, in both cases, who made the decisive moves and salvaged looming defeats, turning the first to a stalemate, the second to victory. Eumenes gained an early advantage in both cases, owing largely to the strength of the Silver Shields. Antigonus kept his cool and watched for his chances. In the first encounter, the Battle of Paraetacene, he launched a quick counterstrike that completely reversed the momentum, then fought his way to a tie. In the second, at Gabene (near modern Isfahan), he devised a devious ploy — one of history's boldest.

In an era without bank accounts or paper money, armies needed to haul their plunder behind them, along with the concubines, wives, and children of the soldiers. Their baggage train thus held the sum of their wealth — considerable, in the case of the Silver Shields — and whatever hopes aging veterans had of a family life and descendants. When battle was joined, baggage trains were secured behind lines or in a nearby city, in hopes the enemy would not get near it. At Gabene, Eumenes left his baggage train largely unguarded, trusting perhaps that his crack troops and trained war elephants would not permit any breakthrough.

But the elephants raised an enormous dust cloud with their heavy tread on dry soil. Antigonus, watching the battle unfold, saw that this cloud offered a screen for his movements. He sent his Tarentines wide of the fray so that, unseen and unchallenged, they penetrated behind the lines and seized Eumenes' baggage train at one stroke. The combat elsewhere was a seesaw affair and the outcome was still unclear when the fighting broke off at dusk. But the Silver Shields were aghast at the loss of their families and fortunes, and angrily turned against their Greek commander. Conspiring with agents of Antigonus, their leaders jumped Eumenes and took him prisoner, then handed him over in exchange for their families and goods.

Here at last we catch a glimpse of Demetrius, though our information is sketchy. While Eumenes languished under heavy guard and Antigonus wavered, Demetrius is said to have pleaded for the prisoner's life, dissenting from the vehement wish of the entire armed camp to see him executed. If this report can be trusted, Demetrius seems to have shared his father's cunning pragmatism: Eumenes, after all, was a first-rate commander and strategist, more valuable as an ally than as a corpse. Or did Demetrius, at age nineteen, feel an unmilitary compassion for a man brought low by a trick in a battle he might well have won?

Whatever his motives, Demetrius failed to convince his father. Eumenes was ordered cut off from food and water; then, when he failed to die quickly enough, a strangler was sent to silently snuff out his life. Antigonus gave his foe honorable cremation, then led his victorious troops back toward the West.

That march quickly became a triumphal procession. The cities of Persia, the heartland of the Asian part of the empire, hailed Antigonus and Demetrius as though they were royalty. The treasury of Susa, from which they had been barred before this, was now thrown open: inside they found astonishing wealth, including the "climbing vine," an age-old statuette of a vine-covered tree done in pure gold. A total of twenty-five thousand talents fell into their hands—a fraction of what Alexander had extracted, but still an amazing windfall, enough funds to pay for an army of forty thousand for more than ten years.

With victories and acclaim, with money to fund their war machine, Antigonus and Demetrius had put themselves far out in front of the contest for Alexander's empire. But that advantage greatly increased their peril. It was almost a law of nature by now that any one leader's success would cause the others to form an alliance against him. Even as Demetrius and his father made their way back from Gabene, their rivals — Ptolemy, Lysimachus, and Cassander, son of the now-deceased Antipater — were reaching out to one another, determined to stop them from raising their heads any higher.

CHAPTER THREE

The Duel with Ptolemy (I)

M any eyes were watching Antigonus and his son with concern, but no one was more concerned than Ptolemy, ensconced in his Egyptian palace — no longer in Memphis but Alexandria, the royal city he built near the mouth of the Nile on a site selected by Alexander himself (and still bearing his name).

Ptolemy knew well what Antigonus meant by creating a Companion Cavalry and having the young Demetrius lead it in battle. He had made his own efforts to evoke the memory and conjure the spirit of Alexander, first by stealing the king's mummified body, then by issuing coins stamped with the image of Alexander, an idealized portrait with flowing hair and the curling ram's horns that signified kinship with Ammon, and finally by writing a memoir of the great anabasis (a work that no longer survives). To a ruler doing his utmost to claim Alexander's mantle, any *new* Alexander — the role for which Demetrius seemed to be cast — was clearly a threat.

Ptolemy's wariness only increased when, shortly after the death of Eumenes, an old friend arrived at his court telling tales on Antigonus. Seleucus, the soldier who helped assassinate Perdiccas, had held a prominent post in One-Eye's administration as governor of Babylon, a crucial strategic stronghold. He had executed his duties faithfully—or so he claimed. But Antigonus had turned mistrustful upon his return from Gabene. He demanded from Seleucus a strict account of Babylon's finances, implying that moneys had been misused. Seleucus refused to present this account, and the dispute had escalated. Seleucus had stealthily fled the city with fifty followers, fearing his life was in danger. Antigonus had sent riders in pursuit, but Seleucus had outrun them and made his way safely to Egypt.

Seleucus had other disturbing accounts of the state of affairs in Asia. Antigonus, now backed by fantastic wealth and strength, had started throwing good men out of leadership posts, and had even executed one former ally. All his arrogance, Seleucus claimed, suggested royal ambitions. The colloquy was much like the one Antigonus himself had taken part in six years earlier when he had journeyed to Europe to tell of Perdiccas's marital plans. The outcome was also remarkably similar. Ptolemy began mustering forces and recruiting allies to fight the Antigonids—both father and son—in Asia; he reached out for help to Lysimachus in Thrace and Cassander in Macedon. A new round of Successor warfare was set to begin, only months after the conclusion of the last.

Ptolemy's coalition presented Antigonus with a set of demands: Seleucus must be restored to Babylon; chunks of Anatolia must be given to Cassander and Lysimachus; and Ptolemy must be ceded control of Syria, the region comprising much of the modern Mideast, especially the coastal cities of Gaza and Tyre, important naval bases. Further, Antigonus must share the wealth he had drained out of Susa, on grounds that all the generals had helped in the war against Eumenes (if only passively) and all deserved part of the spoils. If these demands were met, then equipoise, and peace, could be restored.

Antigonus was having none of *that* balance of power. He had gained the upper hand in the contest and meant to retain it. Dismissing Ptolemy's envoys with scornful replies, he set about recruiting allies of his own. He sent agents to Europe, where civil war was raging, and struck up a pact with Polyperchon, who was vying with Cassander for control of Greece. To further diminish Cassander, Antigonus mounted a propaganda campaign, insisting that this would-be ruler of Macedon was in fact a usurper who had helped poison Alexander the Great—no one was sure just what had caused that man's death—and who was now detaining his rightful heir, Alexander IV, in a kind of imprisonment. The young king and his mother, Rhoxane, were indeed prisoners, living under Cassander's guard in a fortress in Thrace, ostensibly for their own safety. (The other legitimate king, Philip III, was dead by this time.)

Demetrius stood by Antigonus's side during this tense round of diplomacy. Now in his early twenties, he had fathered a second child, a daughter Stratonice, named after his mother. He would have been astonished to learn, as he readied for war with Ptolemy and Seleucus, that one day twenty years hence, this daughter would bear him a granddaughter—*with Seleucus*. Such were the convolutions of the Wars of the Successors, a contest for empire that was often a family feud on a global scale.

It was true, as Seleucus had told Ptolemy, that Antigonus had been purging his officer class, tossing talented men out of posts. He trusted few underlings, especially those like Seleucus who showed unusual talent. His dislike of potential rivals sometimes infected his dreams: One night he dreamed that a certain Mithridates, a Persian nobleman living at his court, was sowing gold dust in the earth, from which sprang golden shoots. Suddenly the shoots were gone and nothing but stubble was left. A voice in the dream said ominously, "Mithridates has reaped the golden crop" — a portent of future dominion. Antigonus resolved to have the man killed.

His plan raised a problem however, since Mithridates was Demetrius's intimate friend, perhaps (according to one recent theory) his lover. Antigonus forewarned his son of the man's coming doom, after first making the boy swear to keep silent. Later Demetrius found himself alone with Mithridates, longing to get his best friend out of danger but unwilling to disobey his father. He stayed true to his oath and did not speak a word, but wrote with his staff in the sand: "Get away, Mithridates!" The Persian escaped and, true to what the voice in the dream had declared, went on to found a new state on the shore of the Black Sea, the kingdom the Greeks called Pontus.

Though that episode had briefly set them at odds, Antigonus and Demetrius enjoyed an extraordinary mutual trust. Plutarch illustrates the point with a brief glimpse of their life together in Celaenae. One day when Antigonus was conversing with envoys from a rival commander, Demetrius came back to the palace from a morning of hunting, walked up to his father, and kissed him, not bothering first to stow his hunting spears. Antigonus called out to the envoys as they departed, "Report this too — that *this* is the state of our family!" It was rare among sovereigns, as Plutarch observes, that a father would let a son approach with lethal weapons in hand.

Well might Antigonus ask that this scene be made known, for paternal trust and filial loyalty were crucial assets in the post-Alexander world. With power so widely diffused and betrayal so profitable, ties of blood or marriage were the only safe forms of alliance, and even these sometimes fell short. As in the Mafia turf wars of modern American cities, "the family" offered stability where other institutions — the state, which had nearly dissolved, and the monarchy, fast disappearing — no longer could. Antigonus understood this new landscape, and thus he had insisted on marrying Demetrius off so young to a woman of proven fertility. With *two* generations of heirs now in place, he could offer the empire a ready-made dynasty.

The empire needed to see not only an heir in the offing, but a strong and competent one. When Ptolemy and Seleucus marched north from Egypt, inviting a showdown in western Asia, Antigonus sent Demetrius to confront them, while he stayed behind to guard against invasion from the north. Like Perdiccas before him, he had to divide his forces for war on two fronts, and he gave his son the critical role, the one more likely to see a head-to-head clash. It was time for the apprentice to start leading troops into battle.

Demetrius went to Gaza, in Syria, with a sizable army: the Companion Cavalry, eight hundred strong, plus more than three thousand other horsemen from various regions; an infantry phalanx of eleven thousand; a thousand javelin men, five hundred slingers, and, his most precious asset, forty-three elephants with their mahouts, a part of the herd Alexander had brought back from India twelve years earlier. These tank-like beasts could break an infantry line by trampling those in their path and also deter an enemy cavalry charge, for horses were unused to their smell and would not approach them.

Though nominally in command, Demetrius was accompanied by a board of senior advisers, men put in place by his father to help him stay out of trouble. All four of these generals had fought under Alexander and knew how to manage a complex, composite army. They had also served beside Ptolemy and Seleucus and understood the prowess of those opponents. When Ptolemy's army arrived—more numerous than their own—they urged Demetrius not to offer battle, but the young man would not back down. He had been taught the example Alexander had set in *his* first show-down with Persia: disregarding the cautions of his father's senior general, Parmenio, Alexander attacked head-on at the Granicus River, and won.

Such bold contempt for the odds showed confidence and dash, qualities that inspired veteran troops. Yet when it came time to rally his men with a pre-battle speech, Demetrius found himself lacking those resources. A huge crowd had gathered, including nearby civilians, to hear what this new and untried commander would say. Demetrius stood on a platform before them, his manner conveying not boldness but nerves and disquiet. A few in the crowd called out to him, trying to buck up his courage, then all fell silent to let the young man speak. At last Demetrius found appropriate, if unoriginal, words, promising spoils and rewards to those who fought well.

Diodorus, our source for this scene, makes clear how much was at stake in Demetrius's onstage debut. The young man's beauty and stature, highlighted by his "royal" armor—the word Diodorus uses here has ironic point, since Demetrius was not yet a king—inspired high hopes in all who beheld him. His temperament had also won him admirers. Diodorus says he possessed *praiotes,* a kind of meekness or mildness, "suitable for a young king," though again he had not become one. Perhaps it was this quality that left him briefly tongue-tied that day as he faced the expectant thousands. His confidence had been shaken in preceding weeks: he had led a flying column of horsemen to confront some of Ptolemy's raiders, and ridden four hundred miles in six days, exhausting his horses, but arrived too late all the same.

The Duel with Ptolemy (I)

In the Battle of Gaza, Demetrius meant to redeem that mistake and establish himself as his father's son and Alexander's true heir. He placed himself on the left wing with the Companions and other cavalry units, as well as the elephants. He planned to deliver a knockout blow against his enemy's right, the place where Ptolemy and Seleucus would be stationed. It was the old cut-off-the-snake's-head strategy, first used by the Thebans sixty years previously to defeat the Spartans at Leuctra, but by now it was well known and easily countered. Ptolemy and Seleucus had foreseen it and built up strength on their right, the place where they knew Demetrius would attack.

The battle began with a close-fought cavalry contest, with all the principal leaders—Demetrius and his co-commanders against Ptolemy and Seleucus—fighting in the forefront. Demetrius got the better of the engagement at first. But Ptolemy, with his superior numbers, was able to outflank and seize the advantage, coming at Demetrius's troops from their unprotected left side. Demetrius had made his wing strong, but not strong enough; in this, Ptolemy had outfoxed him.

Demetrius called in his elephants, expecting that they would tilt the scales in his favor. But Ptolemy had prepared a fearsome iron chain set with spikes, an ingenious device apparently of his own invention. This chain was stretched out so the beasts would step on the spikes and impale their feet. Maddened by pain and harassed by spearmen detailed to barrage them with darts, the elephants began to rampage; their mahouts lost control. The Companion Cavalry sensed the collapse of their wing and fled from the field. Demetrius stayed put as long as he dared, trying to summon them back; in the end he had no choice but to follow. He'd lost.

The battle had been a disaster for Demetrius, but worse was to come. As the survivors retreated past Gaza, Demetrius's base of operations, some entered the city to retrieve the goods they had stored there. Demetrius knew this was no time to stop, but he could not prevent them. Their laden horses and mules clogged the gateway as they hurried out, each seeking not to be last. Then, at the moment of greatest confusion, Ptolemy's pursuit troops arrived. The walls of Gaza could have kept them out, but the gates could not be closed in time with such a throng in the way. Ptolemy gained control of the fortified city, including the baggage train of Demetrius containing the young man's tent and personal effects.

Demetrius rode on with his followers until he reached safety, around midnight, some thirty miles from the battlefield. Here he rested and reckoned up his staggering losses. More than five hundred had perished, mostly cavalrymen from his own elite Companion contingent. The dead included Pithon, satrap of Babylon, and high officers who had fought at Demetrius's side. Other Companions had been taken alive, along with thousands of infantrymen (most of whom had now joined Ptolemy's side) and the entire elephant herd. With glum resignation, Demetrius sent a herald to Ptolemy, seeking a truce under which to gather up corpses — a formal admission of defeat. The high-value prisoners, he foresaw, would have to be ransomed, squandering a huge amount of his family's ready cash.

But then, when his failure seemed total, Demetrius learned that Ptolemy would be generous in victory. The lord of Egypt apparently had no wish to see Demetrius humiliated or to open a breach that could not be healed. He sent back to Demetrius his captured Companions and all his effects without demanding anything in return.

Accompanying the prisoners was a message. "The war between you and me must not be over *everything*, but glory and sovereignty," the message said. It was Ptolemy's way of declaring that this was not a fight to the death but a struggle over rank. He only wanted the balance restored, so that all might coexist as equal partners.

Demetrius accepted the gifts and, implicitly, the terms. He replied that he hoped to soon return Ptolemy's kindness. That seeming courtesy had an obvious double meaning: the favor would be returned when Ptolemy, too, had suffered a defeat.

Demetrius had lost his first solo battle and many of his troops, but he quickly recovered his courage. He sent to his family's forts and garrison posts throughout western Asia, and also to his father in Celaenae, requesting reinforcements on the double. He was determined to fight again at the first opportunity. His showdown with Ptolemy had only begun.

CHAPTER FOUR

Petra and Babylon

The Wars of the Successors are not easily parsed into phases. Some scholars speak of a first, second, third, and fourth "Diadoch War," employing the Greek word that roughly corresponds to "Successor." But ancient historians did not make such neat divisions. The principal chronicler of the era, Hieronymus of Cardia — a name little known today, since his work has been lost — titled his annals *History of the Successors,* taking the men themselves, rather than their conflicts, as his subject. Diodorus, whose work *does* survive, relied on Hieronymus for much of his account of this messy, turbulent era.

In one way, however, the conflict *had* changed in the years after Eumenes' death. A half-dozen leading contenders for power had died, Antipater of old age, the others in battle. One of the titular kings had already been executed; the other, Alexander IV, was a prisoner held by Cassander, and he too was soon to be killed. With the Macedonian kingship increasingly irrelevant and the field of contestants narrowed to four, the struggle became more stable and also more consequential. It was becoming clear by now that whoever came out on top, if anyone did, would exercise total control, without the need to pay court to a meddling monarch.

What did the game board look like after the Battle of Gaza, around 311 BCE? Antigonus and Demetrius held the central position: Asia with all of its riches. Cassander controlled Macedon and much of mainland Greece, having ousted Polyperchon, his chief rival there, from his bases and garrisons. Ptolemy kept a firm grip on Egypt and Cyprus, and now Syria too, for he had taken over Gaza and Tyre after Demetrius's retreat; he was making inroads in Greece as well, in the Peloponnese. And in Thrace, the region today comprising east Greece and southern Bulgaria, Lysimachus, of whom we have heard little so far, had established himself by defeating a Thracian king and overcoming a revolt among the Greek cities of the Black Sea coast.

Antigonus and Demetrius controlled the most territory by far, for their realm stretched far into the East. But such a vast swath was easily cut in two, and that bisection became the goal of their rivals. In the aftermath of his victory at Gaza, Ptolemy gave a small armed force to Seleucus, now his firm ally, and sent him north to fight his way back into Babylon, the city he had recently governed. Seleucus had allies there, and Antigonus had enemies. Gathering more troops en route until he had three thousand, Seleucus took Babylon by storm, ousting the governor who had replaced him. Antigonus sent a force more than three times as large to retake the city, but clever Seleucus hid his men near this force's encampment and fell on it in the night, creating a panic.

With Babylon in his control, Seleucus threatened to take half of Asia away from Antigonus and his son. The garrison troops farther east, as he knew, were more eager to obey a comrade of Alexander who had led them into Bactria and India than an aging one-eyed man who had been left behind in the rear, or a young upstart who hadn't known Alexander at all. Seleucus played on the loyalties of these troops, talking of a dream he had had in which Alexander himself had promised him future dominion. Like all the most ambitious Successors, he sought to portray himself as the favorite, or destined heir, of the vanished god-king. In the contest to win over troops—who could vote, in effect, by defecting from one general to another, as often as they chose—such "dreams" were a potent asset.

Demetrius would in time try to deal with Seleucus, but first he had more to do against Ptolemy, who was pushing farther north in Syria. Restoring his armed strength with fresh recruits, Demetrius returned to the scene of his first battle and his first defeat. This time things turned out differently. Using the same trick Seleucus employed in Babylon (though which came first is unclear), Demetrius took Ptolemy's general, Cilles, completely by surprise in a night attack. He netted seven thousand prisoners, including Cilles himself, without even coming to blows.

With this success Demetrius reversed his Gaza humiliation. He underscored the symmetry by sending Cilles back to Ptolemy unransomed, thus fulfilling his pledge to return Ptolemy's kindness tit for tat. Strange bonds were being forged between these two, mingling bitter rivalry with respect and even a kind of affection. One day, more than twenty years hence, Demetrius was to become Ptolemy's son-in-law.

In Celaenae, Antigonus was cheered by the news of his son's Syrian triumph. He journeyed south to join Demetrius, bringing more troops and an elephant herd with which to pursue the campaign. He had stayed out of the fight long enough for his son to prove himself—this, according to Plutarch, had been his intent. The Battle of Gaza had worried him and prompted a cutting remark, that Ptolemy had beaten only junior contestants, beardless youths, instead of real men. But now Demetrius had won a battle on his own and become a real man. Father and son could stand together as equals.

Ptolemy sized up the new situation in consultation with his staff. The arrival of Antigonus and his elephants meant that the odds were not in his favor in Syria. He took his army back to Egypt and left the place to his foes, first destroying the coastal towns so that Antigonus could not use them. There would be no showdown as yet between these two powers, but one would soon come. Antigonus was already preparing an invasion of Egypt; he had sent an officer, Athenaeus, to subdue the Nabataeans of the Sinai Peninsula. This Arab tribe could help him cross the forbidding desert, if rendered tractable — in their case, by the taking of hostages, the principal goal of Athenaeus's mission.

While preparing to march on Egypt, Antigonus conducted a proxy war against Ptolemy in mainland Greece, the fabled land of Athens, Corinth, and Thebes. These city-states offered fortified bases and, perhaps more important, moral legitimacy. Ptolemy's troops controlled some of them while others were in the hands of Cassander, his ally; Antigonus therefore supported their rival, Polyperchon, and also sent his own nephew to Greece at the head of an army. The hapless Greeks could do little but await the struggle's outcome, hoping to regain their cherished autonomy. Antigonus had promised that if he prevailed, the Greeks would indeed have that back — that is, he would toss out the garrisons installed by Cassander and Ptolemy.

The leading prize of this contest in Greece was Athens, especially its impregnable harbor, Piraeus. Cassander had gained control of both places — effectively two different cities a few miles apart, connected by a walled corridor — and secured them by garrisoning a hill in Piraeus, a site called Munychia. This gave him a choke-hold on the Athenian food supply: cargoes of grain were brought in by ship to Piraeus for transport to the more populous upper city. Cassander held sway politically, too, by way of a supple, re-sourceful puppet ruler whose name — alas — was Demetrius! In no other period of Greek history do we find two such prominent fig-ures who are exact contemporaries and whose names are exact hom-onyms. Historians have distinguished them by calling the leader of Athens "Demetrius of Phalerum," or sometimes "the Phalerite," as opposed to "Demetrius" plain and simple, which always means the son of Antigonus. We'll do the same when we return, in the chapter that follows, to the contest for Greece, which pitted one Demetrius against the other.

In the deserts near Sinai, meanwhile, Athenaeus was making quick work of his mission to subdue the Nabataeans. These Arab nomads were known to use "the Rock," or Petra (in modern-day Jordan), as a place to deposit their families and property when they went to do business at regular market bazaars. Athenaeus launched a quick strike on the Rock, seized hostages and plunder, and left in haste before the menfolk could return. After putting some twenty-five miles between himself and the Rock, he made camp and, thinking himself out of danger, left only a minimal guard. But some of his prisoners escaped as the army slept and found their way to their Arab pursuers, who by this time were near at hand. With the information they gave, the Arabs attacked in the night and slaughtered nearly the entire Antigonid force.

The score was thus even, or so the Nabataeans claimed in a letter they sent to Antigonus, hoping it might deter his retribu-tion. Antigonus replied in mollifying tones. The Arabs, he said, had been fully within their rights to avenge their injury; Athe-naeus had gone against orders in seizing their families. This put the Nabataeans at ease, exactly as Antigonus intended. For he was indeed readying an expedition, to be led by Demetrius, to avenge the death of Athenaeus and get back the lost plunder, both the incense and goods stolen from the Arabs and the money they had taken in turn from the slaughtered army.

Demetrius, now in his mid-twenties, had learned well from his father about the importance of secrecy. Some years before this the two had snuck up together on Eumenes in Iran by crossing a sulfurous desert that no one had thought could be crossed. The Nabataean campaign was to be a replay. Demetrius took a flying force — horsemen and infantry chosen for speed — and gave them three days of provisions, food that did not need to be cooked on all too visible campfires. Then he hurried toward Sinai, following faint paths through the sand rather than using watched roads. He meant to arrive at the Arab stronghold while it was still unguarded. But lookouts spotted his approach and warned the main body of Nabataeans by means of beacons. The element of surprise was thus lost.

Demetrius assaulted Petra for an entire day but found he could make no headway against its strong guard. This first-ever siege by the man who would later be called "the Besieger" was coming to nothing, and in fact had left him exposed to considerable danger. Running out of supplies, with no food or water in sight, he might have been forced to make a rapid retreat with Arab pursuit close behind — or a fresh Arab army cutting off his route home. But he had with him enough force to intimidate his foes, and to show that the desert would not in future protect them.

Aware that they would never be safe if this young man came to harm, the Arabs opened up a negotiation. They offered a truce based on mutual friendship and safe passage out of the region for Demetrius and his men. According to Diodorus, they addressed the young man as "king," a title he had not yet earned but which others seemed eager to give him. Demetrius took the deal; it got him out of a difficult spot with no losses. The siege was called off, and Demetrius headed for home.

Along his route homeward he stopped by the Dead Sea, a place barely known to his people, and observed that from time to time huge blobs of asphalt rose to the surface from the sea floor. These blobs were gathered by locals, who sailed out on rafts of reeds and cut them apart with axes. Like whalers discussing their prey, they referred to the bigger blobs as "bulls" and the smaller ones as "calves." The tarlike substance was sold to exporters as shipping caulk and in Egypt as a vital ingredient for embalmers. Demetrius glimpsed a potential revenue stream for the Antigonid house, and a way to get a return from an otherwise fruitless campaign.

Demetrius proudly gave news of his find when he rejoined his father in Phrygia. Antigonus was intrigued by reports of the tar trade but bitterly disappointed in his son's Nabataean adventure. "You have made the barbarians much bolder by letting them off unpunished," he chastised his son. "They'll think it was not our mercy, but our inability to subdue them, that won this reprieve." Events soon bore out this assessment. When Antigonus sent a squad to build ships on the Dead Sea and collect the asphalt, the Arabs attacked in a fleet of reed rafts, bearing arrows and bows, and shot them all dead.

So not even in this did Demetrius boost his family's fortunes. It was proving difficult for the young man to please his father, but then it was not easy having a father whose ambitions embraced the whole world.

By this time Alexander the Great's only son, Alexander IV, had nearly reached the age of thirteen. He had lived for five years with Rhoxane in the town of Amphipolis in custody of Cassander. By law he was ruler of the unified empire; his regnal years, the system by which official documents were dated, had begun in 316, after the death of his older co-ruler, Philip. Still, no one knew what he looked like or how fit he was to hold power. In some eyes his mixed parentage — half Macedonian royal, half Bactrian tribesman — disqualified him, but others were not so sure. So much had changed in the years since his birth that it was no longer clear who qualified to be king and who did not.

Of all those vying for power, Antigonus was doing the most to stand up for the young monarch's rights. He demanded Cassander release Alexander from what was essentially prison. Perhaps he was only resentful that someone other than himself could use the boy as a pawn, or perhaps he foresaw that only a son of Alexander the Great could hold the empire together. Without a monarchy there was little hope of unity; that was why the Successors all invoked Alexander, by dreams and by coins, by the theft of his corpse, or by bowing down to an empty throne that seemed to contain his ghost, as Eumenes once had done and bid his officers do.

In 311 or 310, just after the Nabataean affair, Antigonus once again championed unity under a monarch whom all would obey. In a treaty forged with Cassander and Lysimachus (ultimately signed by Ptolemy too), it was stated that all four commanders would hold power until the young Alexander came of age in a few years' time. During that brief interlude, the treaty affirmed, the four would have clearly defined territories: Asia would belong to Antigonus, Macedon to Cassander, Thrace to Lysimachus, and North Africa, including Egypt, to Ptolemy. Mainland Greece would stay free, with self-governing cities. The Peace of the Dynasts, as the treaty is called, was an attempt to halt the fragmentation afflicting the empire until the new sovereign could take over and make all whole.

Seleucus was not mentioned in this accord, though he was

now firmly installed as a fifth contestant for power. Babylon, his principal base, lay in Antigonid territory, so it seemed clear that it was up to Antigonus to deal with the interloper. And whatever problems vexed Antigonus tended to land in the lap of Demetrius, who was fitter for active service. The one-eyed man sent his son eastward to oust Seleucus, assigning him a force of four thousand cavalry, ten thousand mercenaries, and five thousand Macedonian infantrymen. He was clearly worried about the East, which was slipping away much faster than he could have expected. Yet he also had plans to counter Ptolemy in the West, so he gave Demetrius orders to hurry back home as soon as the job was done.

This Babylon campaign seemed to go smoothly at first, for Seleucus was out of the city with most of his troops when Demetrius approached. Seleucus's chief officer evacuated the troops who remained and hid them in culverts and streambeds, watching Demetrius without being seen. A few of Seleucus's guards were left in the city to keep control of two fortified towers, where much of Babylon's wealth had been stored. Demetrius stormed the first of these towers and took it, but the second held out stubbornly. With time running short and his father expecting him back, Demetrius left a besieging force and prepared to withdraw.

And here Demetrius made a costly mistake. Perhaps frustrated over the uncaptured tower, or wanting to show his father outsized results — still smarting no doubt from the scolding over the Nabataean campaign — he ordered his troops to strip Babylon bare, amassing all the plunder their horses and mules could carry. The short-term gains were enormous, but, as Plutarch observes, the windfall came at the cost of allegiance. Demetrius had treated Babylon like enemy turf, not like his own territory. He had ceded to Seleucus the role of the city's protector, greatly enhancing his rival's prestige.

So Seleucus retained a toehold in Babylon, the gateway to the East. Antigonus later led an army himself to Babylon and tried, but failed, to dislodge him. Though it galled them to lose such a large swath of Asia, Antigonus and his son eventually turned their backs on the East in order to concentrate on the West, where Ptolemy was always on the move. Could they overcome *that* threat, they might be able to go back to Babylon in greater strength and remove Seleucus's thorn from their side before the wound festered.

In 310 or perhaps 309, Cassander, lord of Macedon and vital cities in Greece, finally took the step that many had feared and a few had desired. He ordered his henchman Glaucias, the guard of the young Alexander IV, to snuff out the life of the last legitimate heir of the Argead house, together with that of his mother, Rhoxane. The murders were performed in secret and the bodies hidden, though later, apparently, the young man's remains were brought to Macedon and interred in a sumptuous tomb. (The tomb was uncovered, intact, in 1978, in the village of Vergina, Greece.)

Two other assassinations brought a firm end to the Argead line. Alexander's sister Cleopatra was dwelling in Sardis, in western Turkey, where Antigonus One-Eye kept her under close watch. When he learned that she planned an escape to Egypt to marry the hated Ptolemy, he had her assassinated. Then Cassander struck yet again, doing away with Heracles, an illegitimate son of Alexander who had made a brief bid for power. The Argead royal line thus came to an end. There could be no pretense any longer that the dynasty that had ruled Macedon for three centuries would continue.

Fourteen years earlier, on the day after Alexander the Great's death, Ptolemy had envisioned a world without kings. He had proposed to the general staff, then meeting in Babylon, that the Macedonian monarchy be ended and Alexander's top generals —

those in the room on that day — form a committee, in effect a board of directors, and jointly administer Alexander's realm. It was they, he asserted, who best understood the demands of governance and who had control of the army, the empire's backbone. It was they who could ensure stability and peace.

What took shape fourteen years later was like a nightmare version of Ptolemy's plan on that day. The generals had indeed taken charge without oversight by a monarch, but they had turned their enormous military talents against one another. Instead of stability, an unending war of all against all had ensued. With no hope left now of a king from the Argead line, no inducement remained to bring the five rivals (counting Seleucus) into a shared commonwealth. If unity could be restored, it would have to come through victory by one over all of the others. That, at least, appears to be the goal that Demetrius and his father pursued from this point forward.

mission yet, the liberation — or as some might say, conquest — of Greece.

As far as is known, Demetrius had never visited Greece, though he had been educated in the Greek classics and taught to revere Athens as the center of higher culture. Now Athens was an essential strategic objective, owing to the superb fortifications and dockyards of its harbor, Piraeus. It was by seizing Piraeus that Cassander had first gained a beachhead in Greece, and he clung to that stronghold tenaciously, inserting a garrison force under command of a certain Dionysius, on the Munychia hill that dominated the town. Demetrius planned to go straight at the stronghold and make a lightning strike on Piraeus, knocking out Cassander's main base with his first blow.

Secrecy and surprise, the special talents of the Antigonids, were essential to the success of this plan. Though he sailed with hundreds of ships, Demetrius did not allow their captains to know their route or their destination for fear that word would leak out, though he gave them sealed orders in case they failed to keep up with his flagship. Demetrius was in sole command of the armada — a tall assignment for a man not yet thirty years old, a cavalryman leading his first naval campaign. He was seeking to prove, as Alexander and others had done before him, that a quick-thinking, cool-headed leader could be just as effective on the sea as on land.

Demetrius counted on the complacency of his foes, for Piraeus was so well protected that few would believe a naval assault could be made there. He stationed most of his fleet at the promontory of Sounion, out of sight of Athens itself, and sailed down the coast with only his twenty best cruisers, steering as though for the island of Salamis. From atop the Athenian Acropolis, the other Demetrius, the Phalerite, observed these ships sailing past but assumed they were friendly vessels in Ptolemy's service. Toward evening, the squadron suddenly changed course and sped toward Piraeus. They were inside the harbor before anyone realized whom they belonged to; there they seized control of the booms that could seal off its entrance. In no time the entire fleet, summoned from Sounion, had followed them in.

On shore, Cassander's soldiers were scrambling to man Piraeus's walls and forts, as the local populace flocked to the scene and sized up the unforeseen conflict. Demetrius stood in the prow of his ship, just offshore, and had his herald deliver a proclamation. His father had sent him, he said, to liberate Athens, by kicking out its oppressors and restoring its ancient freedoms. Some Athenian soldiers who served in Cassander's cause threw down their shields at this news, unwilling to fight against a man who now espoused their own interests. On the headland called Acte, Demetrius's men forced a landing and broke through the sector's perimeter wall. Resistance to the invasion began to collapse.

It was clear to Cassander's garrison troops and their leader Dionysius that the mood of the people was violently swinging against them. They retreated into the Munychia fort, a place from which they could hope to hold out until reinforcements arrived. Demetrius and his men streamed ashore and put a siege cordon around the fortified hilltop. Except for this island of resistance, the port of Piraeus was theirs.

In Athens, a few miles away, the Phalerite and his high command got word of what had happened in the lower city. They recognized that they had been overthrown, for Piraeus controlled the upper city's shipments of food and supplies. Negotiations between city and harbor, conducted by one Aristodemus, produced an agreement: the regime leaders could depart under safe conduct provided they never came back. So one Demetrius left and another took over the reins of government, restoring the votes and privileges of even the poorest Athenians. A change of constitution that the masses deeply desired was thus brought about with little bloodshed in perhaps only two or three days. A grateful citizenry began calling Demetrius *soter*, "Savior," and *euergetes*, "Benefactor," titles normally reserved for deities — astonishing honors for a mortal, but only a foretaste of the adulation to come.

Leaving a strong guard to keep the Munychia fortress surrounded, Demetrius took his armada a short distance south and attacked Megara, where Cassander maintained another garrison. The siege of that outpost took several weeks, enough time for Demetrius, now confident in his control, to turn his gaze from Ares, god of war, to Aphrodite and Eros, the gods of passionate love. For if we can trust Plutarch — our only source for the episode that follows — the young man went on a perilous lark in order to make love to a remarkable woman.

Cratesipolis, "subduer of cities," was one of the leading women of her era, renowned not only for looks but leadership. She married a son of Polyperchon, a talented general, and after her husband was killed in battle she had stayed in charge of his troops. With the help of those forces she governed two vital cities, Corinth and Sicyon, for five years, until Ptolemy took them from her and installed his own garrisons. At the time of Demetrius's invasion she was living at Pagae, near Megara, and seeking a route back into the contest for Greece. A liaison with a dashing and bold conqueror, even one much younger than herself, could provide such a route.

According to Plutarch, Demetrius, while at Megara, received a message from Cratesipolis proposing an assignation. Though the siege was ongoing and enemies lurked nearby, the young man took a small, mobile force and went to Pagae for a night of lovemaking. He pitched his tent far apart from his men to spare Cratesipolis any embarrassment. The tryst was a secret, but word leaked out to partisans of Ptolemy in the region. They closed in on the tent before Cratesipolis arrived. Demetrius learned of the impending attack just in time. He borrowed an old ragged cloak and escaped incognito, but his enemies seized the tent with the money and gear it contained.

Though it might have been off-topic for other historians, to Plutarch, student of human nature, this episode was of keen interest. It revealed what he saw as Demetrius's chief flaws: *akrasia*, or lack of restraint when lust, or other indulgences, beckoned, and *philedonia*, devotion to pleasure. It was these traits, in Plutarch's eyes, that linked Demetrius to Mark Antony, the Roman with whom he is paired in the *Parallel Lives*. Just as Antony squandered his power by dallying with Cleopatra, so Demetrius was liable to set aside duty and yield to alluring women. But Demetrius, Plutarch says, was better than Antony at compartmentalizing: when the time for action arrived, he put aside unguents and perfumes, got out of the coital bed, and girded for war.

Returning to Megara in his ragged cloak, Demetrius soon succeeded in "liberating" the city, then gave his soldiers leave to take plunder. But Demetrius was concerned that the sackers might not spare a sage named Stilpo, a man whom he, and the Greek world generally, admired. Stilpo, trained by a student of Socrates, embodied the virtues Demetrius lacked: self-control, sobriety, resistance to pleasure (though even he is said to have slept with his lovely female student Nicarete). The conqueror had the sage brought to his quarters and asked him (again according to Plutarch) whether any of the troops had robbed him of anything. "No one," Stilpo replied, "for no one has taken my insight." Perhaps he already saw the young man's potential for rule and sought, like Aristotle with Alexander, to bend his soul toward virtue.

With Megara in his control, Demetrius returned to Piraeus, where the fight for Munychia was ongoing. The hill was so steep and so well fortified that Athenians considered it nearly impregnable. It had served once before as a stronghold for an occupying power, Sparta, prompting an Athenian patriot to remark that his countrymen, if they could do so, should tear the hill down with their teeth. Demetrius brought not teeth, but artillery, to bear: torsion-driven *petroboloi*, "stone-throwers," that made quick work of any defenders who mounted the walls, and other mechanical marvels. With numbers on their side, Demetrius's men attacked in relays, keeping up pressure all day and all night. Finally they made a breakthrough in one of the walls. The exhausted defenders surrendered, and their chief, Dionysius, was taken prisoner.

What to do with the fort? Demetrius stood at a crossroads: he had promised Athens its freedom, yet Munychia was a strategic stronghold from which the entire region could be dominated. To his credit, Demetrius stood by his word. He ordered the walls of Munychia pulled down so they could not be used again, by himself or others, to occupy Piraeus and thereby intimidate Athens. That gesture, even more than his democratic reforms, showed the Athenians they had aptly dubbed him Savior and Benefactor. He further promised to restore their naval power, with a grant of ship timber to build new triremes and money to hire rowers. Athens could become a great nation again, as in its glory days, now decades past.

No one understood the impact of these gestures better than Stratocles, a cunning Athenian opportunist. It was he who had lied to the Athenians some fifteen years earlier by telling them they had won a crucial naval battle when, in fact, they had lost. The city held feasts and made sacrifices to the gods in thanks for its restoration. The truth became known two days later when defeated vessels sailed into port, and angry mobs confronted Stratocles. "What harm have I done," he implored, "if for two days you have been happy?" Somehow he survived that episode and now played a leading role in the Athenian Assembly, the bastion of democratic decision making, where policy was set by show of hands.

Riding the wave of joy that surged through the city at the fall of Munychia, Stratocles came forward in the Assembly. He proposed a series of measures that were to have immense impact not only on his own times but on the future course of Europe's political consciousness. He sought to turn Demetrius into a god.

Conquerors and liberators had, in the past century, sometimes been granted divine honors by grateful citizenries. Two Spartan commanders, Brasidas and Lysander, had had festivals and athletic games named after them, events usually devoted to the gods. More recently, statues of living rulers—Philip of Macedon, for example, and Alexander the Great—had been set up in public squares, another break with tradition. The lines between mortals and deities had been blurred by such actions, much to the dismay of the pious. Now Stratocles and his pro-Demetrian faction, ascendant in the Assembly, prepared to erase those lines altogether.

By official decree, Demetrius and his father were awarded gold-plated statues, to be set in the market square beside those of two earlier liberators, the so-called Tyrannicides. No other statues had ever been placed beside those heroes, who had struck with their daggers against an oppressive regime. Gold wreaths of massive weight were awarded to both the Antigonids, and civic honors were heaped on their friends and relations. The epithet "Saviors," a consecrated word, was conferred on both father and son as a kind of official title, and an altar was set up at which the populace could make sacrifice to "the Savior Gods." The names Demetrius and Antigonus, in adjectival form, were plastered everywhere:

on yearly athletic games, on months of the calendar year, on two "tribes," or civic divisions, created for just that purpose (forcing expansion of the monuments and plinths on which these groupings were listed), and on two new "sacred" triremes, ships of state reserved for ceremonial functions.

No decree had explicitly called these men gods, but on any natural interpretation Athens agreed to consider them such. This was a startling move in a city that less than two decades earlier had debated whether Alexander the Great could, within bounds of religious propriety, receive an official statue in a public place. The intervening years had seen Athens ground down by losses and humiliated by an occupier; the common people, the *demos,* had lost all citizen rights. The passions spurred when those rights were returned swept through the demos with the force of infatuation. Demetrius, and his father across the sea, had demonstrated *euergesia* — the power to bring benefit to their subjects. In a world of huge winners and losers, that power was as great as any Olympian's.

Athenian envoys crossed the Aegean to lay the new honors in person before Antigonus, and also to ask him to make good on the benefactions they had been promised. One-Eye could afford to be magnanimous, and he knew what the good opinion of Athens was worth. A friend had once told him to use Athens as a scaling ladder into Greece — that is, as a path of invasion. Antigonus had turned that metaphor in a different direction. A people's allegiance made the best scaling ladder, he said, and Athens was a beacon tower that could, if well treated, send fire signals to the whole world, proclaiming his and his son's good intentions. Now he lived up to those words, sending shiploads of timber, grain, and cash to the Athenians, binding the city to him and his son forever — or so he might hope.

Demetrius had brought off his European campaign with bravado and dash, carrying all before him (except the favors of Crate-sipolis). He tried to extend his gains by bribing the garrison chief of Corinth and Sicyon — Ptolemy's man, Leonides. Could he bring this man over to the Antigonid side, Demetrius would have added two more triumphs to those he had scored in Athens and Megara. But Leonides would not budge, and Demetrius did not have time to besiege him. A summons had come from his father: Ptolemy was again on the move. Demetrius was told to form his Greek allies into a league, a symbol of restored Greek freedom and pride, then sail with a large portion of his fleet against Cyprus. That island had again become too useful a base for Ptolemy's forces. The "liberation" of the remainder of Greece would have to wait.

Demetrius, now thirty years old, and married for a second time — he had taken a new wife in Athens, a highborn woman named Eurydice, thus claiming polygamous privileges — crossed the Aegean again in the spring of 306 to go another round with his nemesis, Ptolemy, lord of Egypt.

CHAPTER SIX

The Duel with Ptolemy (II)

The eastern Mediterranean, shared by Greeks, Phoenicians, and various Anatolian peoples, had been a war zone for two centuries by this time, with few interruptions. The Persians had fought the Greeks for control of the region, then Athens had fought Sparta, then the westernmost satraps of Persia had rebelled against their king and warred for their independence. The harbors and ports up and down the Asian littoral — Miletus, Halicarnassus, Tyre, Gaza — and the islands offshore, Cyprus above all, had each been attacked, some multiple times, and several had been destroyed, as various powers sought to deprive their foes of anchorages. For this realm of islands and coastlines could only be won by a navy, and navies needed places to put to shore and to shelter from storms.

Rhodes alone had escaped largely unscathed from the conflicts. Determined to preserve its trade-based prosperity, the island state was carefully steering a course that would keep it on good terms with all the Successors. It had allied with Antigonus and had supplied him with ships, but also, more recently, had struck an accord with Ptolemy too. Now that those two rulers were at war, the time had come for the Rhodians to choose sides — or so Demetrius thought. He stopped at Rhodes on his way to Cyprus and asked for a squadron of ships, but the Rhodians turned him down, claiming they could not take part in a fight against Egypt. That neutrality would soon cost them dearly.

Demetrius meant to strip away Cyprus from Ptolemy, and from Ptolemy's brother Menelaus, who governed the island. That goal would require all four arms of his military: infantry and cavalry (Menelaus had plenty of each), a navy (for blockading the island and preventing Ptolemy from relieving it by sea), and a siege train (to deal with the high, strong walls of Salamis, the island's principal city). Demetrius had already shown at Megara and Piraeus his effectiveness at using artillery and battering rams to assault fortress walls. But nothing compared with the machine he had now designed, a device that came to embody his boldness and immortalize his epithet "Besieger."

The *helepolis* (city-taker) would be a siege tower on an enormous scale, more than 130 feet high and 65 feet wide on each side, rolled on 12-foot wheels. Its nine stories would be crammed with artillery: catapults near the base that could fire two-hundred-pound stones to break down walls, bolt shooters in the middle stories, and lighter stone hurlers and crossbows higher up to mutilate defenders. Bridges at the top would allow storm troops to climb onto the walls, once the resistance was softened. Its grandeur and scale would terrify the besieged and display to the wider world the ambitions of its designer. With the plan of this new device in his head, Demetrius landed his troops on the easternmost promontory of Cyprus, then made his way inland toward Salamis.

Menelaus was waiting to meet him with twelve thousand infantry and eight hundred cavalry, but Demetrius made short work of this force in a pitched battle outside the city. That drove Menelaus and his men inside their walls, and Demetrius set about getting the helepolis built. Meanwhile a distress call had reached Ptolemy from his brother describing the danger to Salamis and asking for help. While Demetrius's giant machine pounded the walls of the city, Ptolemy readied a fleet and prepared to sail north. At the nexus point of the three continents once ruled by Alexander, the world's two most powerful men prepared to do combat, their third such encounter within eight years.

Ptolemy arrived at Cyprus to find that the situation in Salamis was dire but not yet desperate. Demetrius had recently broken through part of the wall, but night had fallen before his men could enter the breach and invade the city. That night the defenders of Salamis had hurled blazing wood and shot fire arrows at the machines, including the fabulous helepolis. The machines caught fire, incinerating some of the men trapped within. Demetrius had been rocked back on his heels but had not slackened his efforts. The city was still hanging by a thread.

Ptolemy's navy totaled 140 warships, too few to take on Demetrius unless they were joined by the 60 ships of Menelaus, bottled up at the moment in Salamis's harbor. Ptolemy sent his brother an urgent message to get those ships out, past Demetrius's blockade, in any way that he could. But Demetrius either guessed at this plan or learned of it from an informer. He posted 10 warships, the most he could spare, to guard the narrow exit point of the harbor, then summoned the rest of his vessels to ready for battle. He had a slight edge in number of ships, even subtracting the 10 at the harbor entrance. If he used that edge well, he could smash Ptolemy's fleet before Menelaus succeeded in making a breakout.

Demetrius drew up his ships in battle formation, himself on the strong left wing. Ptolemy's ships arrived at dawn, hoping to make a surprise attack but finding they were expected. Ptolemy too had strengthened his left; the left-forward tactic first devised by the Thebans was by now so established that *both* generals chose it, each negating the other's innovation. Each had set a strong left wing opposite the other's weaker right; thus both were likely to win on the left. Then they would turn toward the center in order to roll up the line. The question was who would be first to achieve this goal, and whether the ships of Menelaus would play any part.

Diodorus preserves an account of the battle that seems to have come from an eyewitness, no doubt a participant. Demetrius flashed a gilded shield as a signal to his ships to advance. Arrows and stones flew from both sides as they neared one another, the boatswains called for more speed; then came the shock of collision. Marines swarmed onto the decks of enemy ships wherever contact was made. On his flagship, Demetrius fought hand to hand with these boarders and dodged spears and arrows at the same time. Of the three men protecting him, one was killed and the other two badly wounded, yet the young man fought on, heedless of his own safety. On the opposite wing Ptolemy too was no doubt dealing death to his foes, but our source, whoever he was, observed only one of the two commanders.

Meanwhile Menelaus had sent his best admiral, Menoetius, with orders to break his fleet out of Salamis Harbor and aid Ptolemy. With a six-to-one advantage over the blockaders, Menoetius was sure to prevail, but how long would it take? Demetrius was already smashing the ships he faced, and Ptolemy was doing the same on the opposite wing. Each broke through the line and then turned toward the center, racing to get there first. But as he sailed toward his right Ptolemy saw his own ships breaking formation and running from their pursuers; he arrived just too late. Menelaus's ships by this time had broken free of the harbor, but they too had narrowly missed the crucial moment. By the force of his charge and the strength of his numbers, Demetrius had prevailed.

Ptolemy disengaged and sailed down the coast to safety, then back to Egypt, leaving behind a tremendous number of wrecked and disabled vessels. Demetrius took possession of these, as well as of the support ships that had been too slow to keep up with the retreat. These contained huge troves of money and gear, as well as a woman Ptolemy had brought along with him, a "companion"— that is, a hetaera. This woman, who called herself Lamia after a mythic man-eating monster, was to change Demetrius's life and earn a huge place in Greek lore.

Athens had played a small part in this Salamis triumph, with a contribution of thirty warships and crews. Demetrius rewarded the city by sending it twelve hundred sets of captured weapons and armor, trophies to mount in their temples or combat weapons to distribute to the poor. The gesture echoed a gift made by Alexander the Great, who sent Athens three hundred such panoplies after *his* first victory against the Persians. Demetrius was not only claiming the mantle of Alexander; he was enlarging it by a factor of four. His victory over Ptolemy had put him, and his father, decisively into the lead in the contest for empire.

With no hope left of defense, Menelaus surrendered his city. All Cyprus, complete with its army and navy, fell into Demetrius's hands.

In Syria, Antigonus One-Eye was busy constructing his capital city, Antigoneia, on the river Orontes, when the battle in Cyprus took place. He was anxious for news of his son, and grew even more anxious when he learned that a messenger, the trusty Aristodemus, was making his way to the palace, walking alone from the coast and maintaining total silence. Antigonus sent envoys to intercept him and learn what he had to report, but Aristodemus said nothing, either to them or to the crowd that collected around him as he made his way.

As Aristodemus approached, Antigonus could not hold back any longer. He ditched protocol and went to meet the envoy in person at the palace entrance. A scene took place there that Plutarch depicts as spontaneous but which may have been carefully scripted by Antigonus, then played before a credulous public.

Surrounded by an expectant crowd that included Macedonian soldiers, Aristodemus stretched out his hands and hailed his master with a significant title: "Greetings, *King* Antigonus." Then he reported his news: "We have beaten Ptolemy at sea; Cyprus is ours, along with 16,800 soldiers taken prisoner."

Antigonus, no doubt by design, ignored the man's salutation, though it contained that potent word *king*. Instead he gave vent to annoyance at being kept in the dark for so long: "Greetings to you too; by Zeus, you'll pay for tormenting us like this." But no one had missed the meaning of the envoy's opening words. The crowd took the cue and picked up the language: "*King* Antigonus," people murmured, and "*King* Demetrius" too. These titles had been bestowed on the father and son before, by Arabs and Persians, but now they came from the mouths of the ruling elite.

Some "friends" among the throng, no doubt coached beforehand, produced a diadem—the simple monarchic headband adopted by Alexander—and placed it on One-Eye's head. He did not refuse it. A line was thus crossed that many, not least Antigonus himself, had no doubt thought about crossing for years.

In the message he sent back to Cyprus, Antigonus addressed Demetrius, too, as a king, and sent him a second diadem with which to self-coronate. Just what realm these two men were monarchs of was a question neither one raised and no one, perhaps, could have answered. But at last, seventeen years after the death of Alexander, four years after the extinction of his line, the world once again had a viable royal family.

CHAPTER SEVEN

The Duel with Ptolemy (III)

Whatever the Successors built, they built on a massive scale. Demetrius's helepolis was paralleled by innovations in naval engineering that expanded the standard Greek trireme, with its crew of two hundred, to ships many times as large; Demetrius sailed on a septireme or "seven" in the battle of Cyprus, a newly devised vessel with increased oar power and a vastly greater number of soldiers on board. Thereafter the numbers kept climbing; late in life, Demetrius went to "fifteens" and "sixteens," and a "forty" was seen not long after, propelled by four thousand rowers. Buildings too were becoming giants: the Pharos of Alexandria, a lighthouse commissioned by Ptolemy, stood over three hundred feet high, a beacon broadcasting its builder's magnificence.

Huge caches of wealth, first captured by Alexander and now controlled by his generals, made possible such gigantism; they also allowed the expansion of armies to ever-greater dimensions. Multitudes of men, bedazzled by riches others brought home or robbed of their farms and flocks in the constant fighting, were willing to make a career out of soldiering. The Successors hired, outfitted, and trained these recruits, creating enormous cohorts that fought under their banners — so long as the pay and plunder kept coming. Across the vast empire, hundreds of thousands of soldiers now dwelt under arms in camps, forts, garrisons, and newly built outpost towns, drawing a regular salary, securing their posts, awaiting the orders that moved them from place to place as their generals needed.

Bigger armies exerted more power, but their size was also a drawback, as the Persians had learned long before when invading Greece under King Xerxes. The vast Persian fleet — more than twelve hundred ships, by one count — had been too large to find shelter from storms, and many were lost to the weather; the army, meanwhile, denuded of food any land that it crossed. The failure of Xerxes' invasion led Herodotus, its chronicler, to conclude that the gods despised enormity and would do their best to destroy it. The lightning bolt of Zeus, Herodotus observed, invariably strikes at the tallest trees in the forest.

Antigonus One-Eye and Demetrius had read their Herodotus, as well as the many Greek plays in which jealous gods took revenge on overly grand shows of force. But their successes in Cyprus and Greece, due in part to the scale of their armies and fleets, gave them hope that total supremacy was within their grasp. By making a massive effort they might eliminate Ptolemy, their principal rival, and add a third continent, Africa, to the two they largely controlled. As the year 306 neared its end, they prepared to invade Egypt with 80,000 infantry, 8,000 cavalry, and 83 elephants — the largest land army yet assembled by any Successor — and a fleet of 150 warships and 100 support vessels. They ignored the fears of their captains, who muttered that the Pleiades constellation was already disappearing below the horizon, a sign that the sailing season, when fleets could safely be on the sea, was nearing an end. Antigonus called the men cowards. The time to strike was *now,* he thought, with Ptolemy still unprepared.

The failure of Xerxes in Greece was less on the mind of Antigonus than the failure of Perdiccas in Egypt, some twelve or thirteen years earlier, when in their attempt to recover the body of Alexander, two thousand men had been drowned or eaten by crocodiles while fording a branch of the seven-mouthed Nile. Antigonus knew better than to try that approach a second time. He planned to use the *fleet,* led by Demetrius, to sail past some or all of the mouths of the Nile and land troops on their farther (western) side. Ptolemy would need to draw off men from his Nile forts to meet that threat, allowing Antigonus and the army to ford with small opposition. The land and sea forces, headed by father and son, would operate in tandem to take Egypt by storm.

A force of such size required a staggering store of supplies. Antigonus called on the Arabs with whom he had forged a treaty of mutual aid to meet him in Gaza and bring a camel train. Our sources report that the beasts were forced to haul more than five thousand tons of grain, enough to feed the land army for almost two months. In the end, it would not be enough, as one of the officers, Medius, foresaw in a dream. He dreamed that Antigonus was running a *diaulos,* a footrace of about four hundred yards, accompanied by his whole army. One-Eye started strong but his stamina gave out on the final stretch, and he barely dragged himself across the finish line, panting and wheezing. It was a premonition that resources might fall short.

The army of invasion set out from Gaza in late October 306, marching south through Sinai and dodging its fearsome quicksand pits. The fleet, led by Demetrius, set sail soon thereafter and had several days of fine weather, but then felt the blast of the season's stormy North Wind. Some of the transport ships were swamped, dropping precious artillery pieces into the sea, while other vessels had to run to shore to find shelter. Demetrius pressed on toward Egypt with the rest of the fleet; he arrived there without further losses but then, since the coast was in enemy hands, had to anchor offshore in a heavy swell. For days the boats pitched and heaved as onboard supplies of drinking water dwindled to nothing. At last, when death by thirst was only a day or two off, his father's land army arrived and cleared the beach for a landing.

For Demetrius, who had borne the brunt of the campaign's late start, the ordeal thus far had been harrowing but the losses light. A few quinquiremes (fivers) had been sunk and a few transport ships, perhaps no more than expected. His big test, however, lay ahead, for his father's plan relied on *him* to turn the Nile's defenses. He had to force a landing west of the Nile's mouths or at least within the delta, or else the nearly ninety thousand land troops would be useless, unable to ford.

Those men were already feeling unsure about their prospects. When Ptolemy sent heralds across the Nile in small boats to shout an offer of higher pay to those who would desert to his side, a disturbing number took him up on it. Antigonus drove off the boats with artillery fire, then tortured to death any would-be deserters he caught. It was a cruel measure, but desertions like this could be fatal, as he well knew, having drawn them himself to defeat the wily Eumenes.

In his earlier naval campaign at Athens, Demetrius had made great use of surprise, but along Egypt's wide-open shores, his movements were hard to conceal. Ptolemy's scouts could watch every tack from their lookout posts. In his first attempt at a landing, at a place called Pseudostomon, he found he had been anticipated. Ptolemy's men were ready with bolt shooters as he approached, and the hail of metal projectiles forced him to back off. So he sailed to his next landing point in pitch dark, hoping to find it unguarded. As he had at Athens, he concealed the route from his many ships' captains; he told them only to follow the lantern lit in the rear of his flagship.

But no lantern was bright enough to be seen by all in a fleet of a hundred vessels. Demetrius arrived at his target to find that many ships had gone off course in the night. He sent a fast cruiser to round them up, but this took time, and as he delayed, Ptolemy's troops came streaming to the place where he hoped to make landing. By the time he felt he was ready, the shore was bristling with soldiers and fearsome artillery weapons. Demetrius backed off again. He had lost what the Greeks called *kairos*, the opportune window of time – exactly the thing Alexander the Great had always managed to seize.

On his way back toward his father, Demetrius felt the wind once more veer around to the north. That steepened the waves and drove his ships toward the shore, where Ptolemy's men were eagerly waiting to seize them. As he watched from his tossing flagship, a few ran aground and became part of Ptolemy's navy, their marines part of Ptolemy's army. Not many were lost, but enough to add an extra sting of humiliation to his two failed landing attempts.

On land, the vast host led by Antigonus had spent weeks waiting to go into action, consuming supplies all the while. Food was by now running short. The army was useless without the success of the navy, and now the navy was blocked. Antigonus called a solemn assembly at which to consider the options. His officers overwhelmingly felt it was time to go home; they would try the invasion again at a time when the Nile was lower and easier to ford. Ninety thousand men and countless camels and mules turned around and marched glumly back through the desert, with the fleet sailing alongside. The greatest invasion force assembled by any European commander had not accomplished a thing.

In Egypt, Ptolemy celebrated the strength of his Nile defenses, which had twice now defeated attempts at penetration. The province of Egypt, he claimed, was "spear-won land," legitimately his by recognized laws of war. At around this time, following the model Antigonus had set, he proclaimed himself king, or, in local terms, pharaoh. He sent letters to the other Successors—Cassander, Lysimachus, and Seleucus—informing them of his success and boasting of how he had drawn deserters from Antigonid ranks.

Antigonus and Demetrius had aimed at sole monarchy, donning crowns that implied control of the three-continent empire. But now, after failure in Egypt, it seemed they would have to share the royal prerogative. They had struck hard at Ptolemy but ended by making him stronger and giving him an opportunity to also self-coronate. It seemed the struggle for empire was destined to last a lot longer, and get more complicated, than anyone might have expected at its start.

straddling of the line, Antigonus and Demetrius decided. The Rhodians would have to choose sides.

Antigonus began with a measured provocation: he sent a squad of ships to interdict the robust Rhodian trade with Egypt. The Rhodians drove that squad off, so Antigonus stepped up the pressure by threatening war. This made the Rhodians fearful. They tried appeasement, voting high civic honors to Antigonus and Demetrius, and vowing, by way of envoys, to support the Antigonid cause—in anything except a fight against Ptolemy. This exception only made Antigonus more angry, and he sent Demetrius to the island with troops and siege engines. The issue would, it seemed, be decided by force of arms.

With Demetrius setting up base on the mainland just off their coast, the Rhodians compromised further, vowing to fight for the Antigonids even against Ptolemy. But Demetrius had learned from his father how to raise stakes. He now demanded the handover of a hundred hostages from leading families to serve as guarantees of compliance, as well as the right to bring his ships inside the island's main harbor. If it complied with either demand, Rhodes would forfeit its treasured autonomy. Demetrius was once again imitating Alexander, who had similarly bullied Tyre, another well-fortified island. First he had asked leave to enter the place with troops to visit the shrine of Heracles. When that request was refused, Alexander conducted a seven-month siege that showcased his iron resolve. Ultimately he prevailed and destroyed the city.

Technology was Demetrius's strong suit and his greatest resource against Rhodes. He never could get enough of the pleasure, says Plutarch, of gazing on the vastitude of his building projects, particularly siege machines: "His works conveyed a certain loftiness of thought and conception. Their scale terrified even his friends, and their beauty gave pleasure even to his enemies." He had built the world's first helepolis during the siege of Salamis; that device had been set on fire by his foes, but Demetrius had learned from his mistakes. Rhodes could give him a chance at a second, successful show of massive mechanical force.

As though following Tyre's example but hoping for a better outcome, the Rhodians refused to grant Demetrius's demands. Both sides prepared for a siege.

To limit the drain on food supplies, the Rhodians sent away any foreigners unwilling to take up arms, as well as (presumably) most women, children, and elderly. This left seven thousand freeborn men fit for combat, together with an unknown number of slaves, who were freed for the upcoming struggle. Measures were passed to ensure that any who died would be buried at public expense and their children and parents provided for by the state (if any "state" was left when the struggle was over). The wealthy donated funds to augment the treasury. Everyone set about building weapons of war, repairing and heightening walls, and seeing to the riggings of ships in various harbors. Envoys were sent out to Ptolemy, Lysimachus, and Cassander enlisting the help of the anti-Antigonid league. According to a surviving Rhodian inscription, the message to Ptolemy was dictated by Athena herself in a dream that appeared to a Rhodian named Callicles.

Meanwhile, at Loryma, a town about fifteen miles from Rhodes, Demetrius was assembling another immense armada, even larger than the one he had brought against Egypt. By the summer of 305 he had amassed two hundred warships and nearly as many troop carriers (this second group able to transport forty thousand armed men and hundreds of cavalry horses). He too had enlisted allies to aid his cause: the privateers and pirates who hated Rhodes for its control of their sea lanes now joined the effort to destroy it. They were confident about Demetrius's chances and hungered for the spoils that the sack of Rhodes would produce. Merchants and profiteers flocked to the scene, all eager to plunder or to trade for the food and supplies that a vast field army required.

The sight of a huge flotilla making its way toward Rhodes one morning in midsummer brought terror and dread to the Rhodians. This was the greatest naval assault seen in the Aegean since the time of King Xerxes. Those standing atop the walls of Rhodes could perhaps make out the artillery pieces on the ships' decks: catapults, stone throwers, and fearsome *oxybeleis,* which fired twenty-eight-inch metal bolts at long range. Such weapons, driven by bundles of hair wound taut and then released, were the newest innovations in naval warfare; mounted securely on prows, they could target troops on shore or atop city walls, or drive off approaching enemy vessels. Demetrius employed a team of crack engineers who were constantly improving these machines.

Also in Demetrius's employ was an expert armorer by the name of Zoilus. Working on Cyprus, an island now in Antigonid hands, Zoilus devised two iron breastplates so astonishingly strong that a catapult bolt fired from fifty feet away dealt them only a faint scratch. Demetrius of course got one of the pair; the other went to an officer, Alcimus of Epirus. This sturdy, stalwart soldier is said to have regularly gone into battle bearing over a hundred pounds of infantry gear.

Demetrius needed such technical know-how to overcome Rhodes's defenses. The island's main city was served by two deep-water harbors, the main one partly enclosed by a jetty and able to be fully sealed by a floating boom. The city itself sat on a promontory, where a rough coastline protected much of its perimeter; in spots that could be approached by land the Rhodians had erected high, stout walls. Even the seagirt sector was walled, though not as strongly as the parts facing inland; the Rhodians trusted the jetty and boom to keep foes away from those ramparts. Demetrius planned to force his way past the harbor defenses, as he had done at Athens, and thus gain access to this weaker section of wall, while also patrolling the whole coast to interdict shipments of food. If he could not take the city by force, he'd starve it into submission.

But to gain control of the harbor entrance was a formidable task. In an age of swiftly advancing artillery weapons, the Rhodians had constructed long-range bolt shooters, capable of reaching the harbor entrance from atop the walls. Demetrius needed protection from these if he was to approach the jetty. He built two wooden shells he called tortoises, ship-mounted pillboxes to shield his men from artillery fire while they rowed up to the harbor and (if they got that far) the city itself. These tortoises were so enormous that two warships lashed together were needed to carry each one.

Two other yoked pairs of ships bore enormous siege towers. These could be rowed right up to the walls once artillery fire from the tortoise-bearing ships — gunships, in effect — had cleared them of defenders. Several smaller vessels were also converted to gunships, to support this group of four behemoths. To protect the whole squadron from Rhodian naval attacks, Demetrius devised an ingenious defense shield: a device consisting of floating logs linked together by spike-bearing chains, stretched out in a circle around the flotilla. Any ship trying to ram the yoked ships would drive into the spikes and pierce itself through the hull.

All this took shape at the point on the Rhodian coast where Demetrius had established his camp and his own makeshift harbor. The Rhodians learned through spies and informers what was coming their way, and they took their own countermeasures: they built tortoises of their own on the jetties and converted some ships into gunships. The Rhodians meant to lay down enough artillery fire to prevent penetration of the harbor. In case that effort failed, they had stationed a set of gunships in a second harbor, normally used by trade vessels. They planned to bring these to bear on the rear of the Antigonid convoy if it got through to their walls.

Demetrius started his attack at night, both for secrecy's sake and because the seas were calmer then (an earlier, daytime effort had nearly been swamped). His initial approach was a stunning success. Troops landed by the advance ships seized the end of the jetty at a point about five hundred feet from the city and set about fortifying the place with stones and wood planks. A squad of four hundred artillery men was then inserted, with enough ammunition to cover the harbor entrance. Then the great convoy of paired siege vessels was towed to the harbor, reaching it around daybreak. With shouts and the blowing of trumpets, these eight yoked ships bearing tortoises and siege towers advanced toward the city wall and assailed it with stones and catapult bolts, causing significant damage.

But the Rhodian artillery crews had prepared by placing plenty of bolt shooters in range of the harbor. Their counterfire proved heavier than the attack ships could withstand, and Demetrius had the ships towed back out of range as night approached. As they retreated the Rhodians tried to set them ablaze, using small fire boats filled with dry wood covered in pitch. But this effort—modeled no doubt on a similar tactic used at Tyre against Alexander—did not succeed.

The seaborne assaults went on for eight days, while Demetrius's infantry assaulted the walls on the city's landward side. Finally Demetrius knocked out the Rhodian tortoises and brought his siege ships up to the damaged walls. For hours, the fate of Rhodes hung in the balance, as the attackers on both land and sea set scaling ladders and began to mount the walls. But the Rhodians fought with the desperation of those on the brink of annihilation. They drove back the scalers and captured a few high-ranking officers who had been first to climb up. They landed firebombs on some of the ships, especially those which had grounded themselves on jagged underwater rocks. Demetrius once again was forced to withdraw.

After a weeklong hiatus to repair his damaged equipment, Demetrius renewed his assault, this time also using fire arrows against Rhodian ships anchored in the main harbor. These had stood idle thus far, deterred by the floating spiked chain, but now the Rhodians put them to use. After dousing the flames the arrows had kindled, they manned three ships with their best rowers and by repeated ramming managed to break through the chain. The siege ships inside it were helpless against the more maneuverable Rhodian vessels. Demetrius watched as two of the pairs were rammed below the waterline, listing perilously as they filled with water. He managed to tow the last seaworthy pair out of harm's way (a fourth pair had already been beached or destroyed by this time). A Rhodian ship pursued it too hotly and ended up captured.

The struggle had gone on in seesaw fashion for two or three weeks at this point, and Demetrius was losing patience. The failure of his paired siege ships was costly and embarrassing, but a greater embarrassment was soon to come. Relying as usual on gigantism to tilt the odds in his favor, Demetrius fitted out an enormous siege ship with a tower triple the size of his initial models. This leviathan was meant to terrify the Rhodians and make short work of their walls. But as it was being towed toward the harbor, a southerly wind sprang up and the seas became rough. With so much weight on its deck the great battleship was unstable, and it simply toppled over and sank without ever striking a blow.

Perhaps, Demetrius must have thought, Herodotus was right when he wrote that the gods hate big things. In the Persians' attack on Greece, as told by that author, a sudden North Wind, called

Boreas by the Greeks, had destroyed a part of Xerxes' invasion fleet. This time the South Wind, Notus, had helped to even the scales of battle, and it wasn't done with him. The rough seas it had kicked up prevented Demetrius from sailing to the harbor in force. The Rhodians seized the moment and stormed the artillery fort on the end of their jetty. With no reinforcements arriving, all four hundred of Demetrius's men were forced to surrender. The Rhodians had taken back their harbor entrance.

Thus far the Rhodians had fought alone against Demetrius, but now, with the fall of the jetty fort, they could again risk sorties to contact allies elsewhere or bring in supplies to support the defenders. Ptolemy was their main source of such resupply. Early on in the siege, he sent five hundred soldiers to help protect Rhodes, among them many Rhodians who had signed on to serve him in Egypt. This relief force was rowed into the harbor past the Antigonid ships and landed near the gates of the city, then smuggled inside. Demetrius had failed in his principal task, maintaining a cordon to cut Rhodes off from the world. With Ptolemy now lending aid, the siege was sure to be long.

Other Successors were also at work, taking advantage of Demetrius's difficulties. Cassander was still determined to dominate Greece. He had been booted out of Athens and Megara, but seeing Demetrius bogged down in Rhodes, he was back on the move. A decade earlier he had made allies among the Boeotians by restoring their principal city, Thebes — a place destroyed by Alexander the Great. With a secure base not fifty miles from Athens, Cassander had started making inroads toward that "beacon" city, hoping to once again install his garrison troops. The Athenians, who had kicked out Cassander's men the previous year, were at grave risk with their "Savior" so far away.

Seleucus, too, was seizing the opening offered by the stalemate at Rhodes. Unafraid for the moment of an attack from the west, he turned his attention eastward, toward the region the Greeks called India (today largely Pakistan). A powerful king, Chandragupta Maurya, had taken over this realm and ousted the Macedonian overlords appointed by Alexander. Seleucus wanted the province back, to harvest its riches but also, especially, to export its most precious (in his eyes) resource: trained war elephants and their mahouts. He invaded the region in force (in a campaign about which little is known). Ultimately he was to fail in his quest, but he did gain a vast herd of elephants for his efforts—much to Demetrius's later woe.

Watching all this play out from his new capital in Syria, Antigonus One-Eye and his court waited for news with mounting concern. Demetrius's ships and machines should have made short work of the siege, they expected, but as weeks and then months rolled by, and winter arrived, it was clear that something was wrong.

In Cilicia, where she had taken up residence, Demetrius's wife Phila was also growing anxious. With tender concern for her husband's comfort and pride, she prepared a royal care package—new purple robes and soft bedding—and sent it by ship to Rhodes. Despite Demetrius's polyamorous ways she remained a devoted wife as she raised the couple's two children, Antigonus Gonatas, the heir to the heir to the empire, and his younger sister Stratonice.

CHAPTER NINE

Assault on Rhodes (II)

Despite all Demetrius could do, the harbors of Rhodes still allowed relief shipments in and Rhodian sorties out. The expert captains and rowers of Rhodes had formed commando squads during the time of the siege and disrupted Antigonid supply lines with phenomenal success. They had sunk, torched, or captured numerous vessels, seized precious food shipments, and made prisoners of officers and crews all around the Aegean. These captives had to be ransomed to Demetrius for a set price, as agreed in a compact arranged before the siege started. But when the Rhodians seized eleven military engineers, they refused to abide by the pact; such men were too dangerous to be given back to their foe.

One day a Rhodian captain, Menedemus by name, was cruising off Lycia on the Turkish coast when a remarkable prize fell into his hands. He had already had a good outing – burning one ship found riding at anchor and capturing numerous freighters – when he spotted a quadrireme making its way from Cilicia. After getting control of the ship, he seized its fabulous cargo: the purple robes sent by Phila to her husband, together with private letters and other royal effects. The ship's crew were sold into slavery, but the robes and gear seemed too fine to be merely converted into cash. Judging that only a king ought to wear such an outfit, the Rhodians sent it to Ptolemy, now also a king.

That gesture was sure to enrage Demetrius, but, strange to tell, the Rhodians did not hate their attacker, or at least did not show it. When in an Assembly meeting someone proposed pulling down the city's statues of Demetrius and his father, the citizens voted to censure the man who sponsored the motion and leave the statues in place. No doubt they were partly moved by fear of what awaited them if they lost, but they might also, perhaps, have felt a strange kind of loyalty. Despite the presence of eighty thousand attackers outside their walls, they were still, in theory, allies of the Antigonids. By honoring that alliance, says the chronicler Diodorus, they won the admiration of Greece and made Demetrius look cruel and ungrateful.

The winter of 305–304 went on with no break in the stalemate, and no sign that the Rhodians were weakening in their resolve. Recognizing that their harbor wall might be shaken to pieces, they set about building a second wall behind it, demolishing their theater and even some temples to gain building stone. That way, if Demetrius succeeded in breaking through, he would confront yet another task as formidable as the first. When they learned that sappers were tunneling under the walls, they dug a mine of their own that met up with that of the besiegers. The result was another stalemate: each side posted guards at its end of the tunnel so that neither could use it.

Demetrius, too, only hardened in his resolve as the time went by. He remained convinced that overwhelming force and giant constructions could overcome any resistance. The example of Alexander at Tyre was ever before his eyes: in a seven-month ordeal,

Alexander had used every contrivance, even building a causeway from the mainland so siege engines could be rolled into position. With thousands of tons of rock and fill, he changed the very geography of Tyre, making it a peninsula instead of an island. Eventually he had prevailed. His causeway remained in place, a monument before all the world of the strength of his will.

Demetrius set out to build a similar monument. In his camp outside Rhodes, he constructed a second helepolis, bigger and better protected than the one that had burned down on Cyprus. Its dimensions are variously reported, but it seems to have had a height of 150 feet. Inside it had two stairways, one up and one down, for soldiers to take their stations within its nine stories. At the base an ingenious system of pivots allowed it to move in any direction, pushed by a squad of thirty-four hundred men selected for strength (presumably they worked in relays). Metal plates covered its surface on three sides to repel fire missiles, and each opening had its own shutter of stuffed leather cushions, designed to absorb the impact of catapult stones. In case any flaming arrows got through, each story had vessels of water at the ready—an early example of fire extinguishers.

Magnificent as this machine was, Demetrius did not stop there. He also built two giant battering rams, each worked (according to Diodorus) by a team of a thousand men. These rams were encased by enormous tortoises against artillery fire, and eight more tortoises protected the men who would mine under the walls to weaken their foundation. To move all these devices into position, Demetrius had a pathway nearly half a mile wide cleared and made level. From their walls the Rhodians watched in awe as these efforts took shape, but still held on tenaciously to their hopes.

Meanwhile a small drama of double-cross played out at the tunnel exit inside the city. The captain in charge of guarding that portal, a man named Athenagoras, was not a Rhodian but a mercenary soldier from Miletus, one of the forces sent by Ptolemy. Using agents sent through the tunnel, Demetrius bribed him to betray Rhodes and allow a squad of soldiers to move through the tunnel at night. Athenagoras took the bribe and vowed to let one of Demetrius's generals through to conduct reconnaissance. But then he informed the Rhodian council of what was about to take place. The general was seized as soon as he came through the tunnel. The Rhodians awarded a huge cash bequest to Athenagoras, showing to all that loyalty had its rewards.

The resistance of Rhodes was becoming a cause célèbre throughout the Aegean. Not only Ptolemy but Cassander and Lysimachus began sending grain and beans to the besieged, hoping to embarrass Demetrius. Somehow these supply ships nearly always managed to reach their destination. Perhaps Demetrius had too few men to build his enormous siege weapons while also maintaining a difficult naval blockade. When he tried to intercept Ptolemy's grain ships, the winds once again turned against him. As in Egypt, his efforts at sea seemed always to falter, so he looked to the land, where the mighty helepolis loomed, as the place to decide the long struggle.

When all the machines and the roadway were ready, Demetrius ordered a full-bore attack from both land and sea. The rams and the helepolis lumbered into position while the towering siege ships were towed once again into the main harbor. A fearsome battering and artillery barrage began to shake both landward and seaward walls. Just then, however, a team of diplomats intervened. Envoys from Cnidus arrived at Demetrius's camp and vowed to convince the Rhodians to surrender. No doubt aware of the public relations cost of ignoring such efforts, Demetrius called a halt. In the end, though, negotiations proved fruitless — but gave the Rhodians time to prepare their riposte.

Demetrius recommenced his assault on the walls. He succeeded in shattering one defensive tower and a portion of the adjoining curtain wall. The next day, it seemed, would bring a complete breakthrough. But the Rhodians took advantage of the intervening night. While most of the enemy slept, they suddenly rained artillery fire on the helepolis and the soldiers who came to defend it. Barrages of stones shook loose the machine's iron plates and fire arrows struck the wood planks beneath. The water reserves proved too meager to put out the blaze, and Demetrius ordered the trumpet blown to assemble the pushing squad. As catapult bolts continued to strike — some fifteen hundred in total, according to a count made the next day — the great wheeled device was rolled back out of range to prevent its destruction. Demetrius had to call another halt to repair his machines and tend to his dead and wounded.

The Rhodians, meanwhile, threw up another interior wall, a crescent with its horns attached such that all the damaged parts of the curtain were covered. They dug a moat between these two walls; if Demetrius punctured the first, he would not easily bring his great rams to bear on the second. All these defenses must have required destruction of more public buildings and homes, but that no longer mattered to the Rhodians. If the people survived and no buildings stood, Rhodes still existed, but it ceased to exist if its people were butchered, no matter how many structures remained intact.

With his machines back in service, Demetrius again rolled up to the wall and began to hammer away. Two portions were soon knocked to pieces, but the tower that stood between them did not fall, and from it the Rhodians sent down a hail of artillery fire. A desperate fight for that tower went on a long time. Many Rhodians lost their lives, including the city's leading general. In the end, though, the tower remained in Rhodian hands. Meanwhile, on the seas, Rhodian raiders continued to score win after win, seizing grain ships bound for their attackers and rowing them at night past Demetrius's highly porous blockade.

At some point in this late stage of the operation, Demetrius either captured, or threatened to capture, a precious work of art: a painting of Ialysus, the mythic founder of Rhodes, by the island's grandmaster, Protogenes. This man had such virtuosic skill that an image he made of a partridge was said to have spurred other partridges to sound their mating call. He had toiled on the *Ialysus* for seven years, and the Rhodians were horrified at the thought that the painting, given its subject, might become the target of Demetrius's wrath. They sent an envoy to plead with him not to burn it (or, in another version, not to attack the building in which it was housed, which might result in its burning). The Besieger had no such intention. "I'd rather destroy the statues of my own father," Plutarch quotes him as replying. The painting survived the war and was shown at Rhodes for centuries thereafter, then brought to Rome, where, at some point before Plutarch wrote, it finally burned anyway.

The siege of Rhodes had by now stretched on for eight or nine months and no end was in sight. The total commitment of Demetrius's forces to this one contest inevitably meant his positions elsewhere were eroding, especially in Greece. A delegation of Demetrius's Greek allies arrived outside Rhodes and tried to mediate an end to the siege, but neither side gave much ground. Demetrius felt that thus far bad luck had blocked him, not a failure of strategy. The Rhodians, for their part, had become the darlings of the

anti-Antigonid powers and kept receiving support from three quarters at once, Ptolemy, Cassander, and Lysimachus. The latest convoy
from Egypt had brought them a squad of fifteen hundred trained
Macedonian troops, along with yet more food supplies and weapons of war. Negotiations again came to nothing.

Demetrius had succeeded in creating a small breach in the landward wall, and the Rhodians posted a guard to seal off all access.
Nonetheless, Demetrius gambled that in a night operation, he
might insert troops in enough force to seize a part of the city. Their
penetration would draw off Rhodian strength from the walls and
allow his other squadrons, on sea and on land, to attack unopposed.
The timing would be dicey; the inserted force would need to hold
out long enough to allow their comrades outside to achieve a breakthrough. He selected his strongest and bravest men, fifteen hundred in all, for the mission, including Alcimus, he of the hundred-
pound gear, one of the force's two senior officers.

In the middle of the night this crew of commandos crept to the
breach and overpowered the guard. They made their way inside and
got to the theater district, now ravaged by the quarrying of stones
for the walls, and prepared to defend themselves against enemies
on all sides. Panicky cries were already echoing through the dark
streets, and Rhodians were racing about in disorder — exactly as
Demetrius had hoped.

Outside the walls and in the harbor, Demetrius's forces were
moving into position, preparing to launch a hoped-for final assault.
At dawn they saw the flag of battle raised and sent up a great war
cry, loud enough to be heard by their comrades inside the city. Those
men, they knew, were now surrounded by foes and sure to be destroyed if a breakthrough could not be achieved.

Demetrius counted on the Rhodians to lose their nerve when
they saw his men in their midst. But the city had been at war for

nearly a year now, and nerves had been steeled. The city council gave orders for troops on the walls and harbor fortifications to stay at their posts at all costs. The forces remaining, augmented by Ptolemy's latest crew of professionals, would have to be enough to take on the intruders.

And so they were. Though the commando squad kept formation and beat back constant attacks, they could not hold out forever against superior numbers. The Rhodians fought with the zeal of men whose very existence was at stake. Alcimus, the squad's co-commander, finally succumbed to his wounds, and the unit started to crack. Some ran for the breach, and a few of these made it back out alive; the rest were either killed where they stood or captured by the Rhodians, who could not have shown them much mercy.

The grand gambit had failed, but still Demetrius did not lose hope. With the forces he had in place success was surely a matter of time—but time, as he learned, had run out. In the spring of 304 a message arrived from his father, one he must have long dreaded. Events in Greece were spiraling out of control; Cassander had seized border forts in Attica and might retake Athens. Demetrius had to give up the siege and agree to negotiation. The efforts of eighty thousand men and their giant ships and machines over an entire year had come to nothing.

A treaty parley, arranged by Aetolian envoys, hammered out terms of the stand-down. The Rhodians agreed to turn over one hundred hostages, something they had refused to do previously, and become allies of the Antigonids in any fight—except against Ptolemy. The hostage concession provided Demetrius with the barest of face-saving gains, but he still had not won his main point. For his part, Demetrius guaranteed to Rhodes its autonomy and exemption from taxes. The island could trade and prosper as it had in the past, especially by trading with Ptolemy, the Antigonids' nemesis.

While Demetrius dismantled his siege engines and recaulked his ships, the Rhodians paid due reverence to those who had helped them survive. Statues went up of Cassander and Lysimachus, joining the still undisturbed images of Demetrius and his father. But the highest honor went to Ptolemy. A team of *theoroi*, envoys deputed for sacred missions, was sent to the oracle of Ammon in the North African desert to ask whether Ptolemy ought to be seen as a god. The answer was yes. The Rhodians built a fine public square in their city center and called it the Ptolemaeum. They considered Ptolemy their soter, and the epithet stuck firmly: the king of Egypt was known throughout the rest of his reign, and is still known today, as Ptolemy Soter.

Demetrius too had been designated Soter by the Athenians, but at Rhodes he earned his more lasting epithet, Poliorcetes, Besieger. His siege operation there was the biggest and longest seen to that point; it astonished the world with its grandeur and scale. All the same, it had been unsuccessful. The Antigonid giant had stumbled a second time in three years, at the Nile and at Rhodes. Across Alexander's empire, in garrison forts, army camps, and councils of state, all those taking part in the Successor struggle had to make new calculations. The odds that Demetrius could win in that struggle and be a new Alexander, holding the world in his grasp, had fallen considerably.

Demetrius packed up his gear and headed for Greece, but the great helepolis, unlike smaller siege machines, was not designed to be taken apart and transported. It had to be left outside the walls of Rhodes, a monument to the determination of both the city's attackers and its defenders. A story was later told — perhaps true — that the Rhodians sold off the parts and raised three hundred talents, with which they funded their famous Colossus, erected some three decades later. However they paid for it, the hundred-foot statue of Helios, patron god of the island, was certainly meant to express the Rhodians' pride in their courage and stamina, and also, perhaps, to tweak the nose of Demetrius — who was still on the scene at the time it was planned.

Demetrius's failure at Rhodes emboldened his rivals. Up to now, the Antigonids and Ptolemy had proclaimed themselves kings, but soon after Rhodes, the other Successors — Cassander in Macedon, Lysimachus in Thrace, and the latest contestant to enter the competition, Seleucus in Babylon — did so as well. The empire of Alexander now had five crowned heads in five domains, as well as a free zone in Greece where city-states, principally Athens, theoretically governed themselves in their time-honored fashion.

Demetrius and Antigonus laughed at these new assertions of monarchy. The courtiers of Demetrius pleased their sovereign by refusing to call his rivals kings and instead awarding them mocking, insulting titles. But in a world where crowns could emerge ex nihilo, the father and son who first took them were helpless to stop their proliferation. These two were still in the lead in the game of global dominion, but the others were catching up fast.

CHAPTER TEN

Demetrius the Descender

Life was unstable and rough for Athenians of the late fourth century BCE. Athens, the "school of Hellas" in the previous century (as some had termed it), still enjoyed an august reputation as the home of Pericles, Demosthenes, and Phocion. But by now all those men were dead, and no comparable leaders had taken their place. The city had changed allegiance multiple times in a very short span, as one general after another—Philip, Alexander, Antipater, Cassander, Demetrius—brought it under his sway. Purges and banishments had gotten rid of the oligarchs, then the democrats, then the oligarchs again, as the constitution veered back and forth between rival political systems. Yet life for most Athenians went on in the usual way, as seen in the pleasant comedies of Menander, composed at this time.

When Demetrius stormed Piraeus in 307, the Athenians had placed all their bets on the Antigonid house. Following the lead of Stratocles, the Assembly had practically divinized Antigonus and his son and had thrown out the partisans of Cassander, their former occupiers. At the time this had seemed a prudent move, but then came Egypt and Rhodes. Nervous Athenians watched as Cassander's troops made their way closer, ultimately seizing two forts on Attic soil. To their south, most of the Peloponnese was already in the hands of Cassander's leading general, Prepelaus. Hence their impatience with the siege of Rhodes, which dragged on endlessly as danger to Athens grew.

Antigonus had called Athens a beacon, able to broadcast his family's virtues to all the world. He cast himself and his son as champions of Greek freedom, and in truth they had supported a far more liberal line than their rivals. Cassander had garrisoned nearly every city he took, using armed force to exert control; the Antigonids vowed to remove those tools of oppression and let the Greeks govern themselves as of old. The Antigonids logically assumed that autonomous cities would support their liberators, so the cry of "freedom for Greece" was in their own interest. As with so many moves in these times, noble motives are hard to discern, yet many Greeks, especially the Athenians, held a high opinion of the one-eyed man and his son, whom they had designated their Savior Gods.

Demetrius was a favorite in Athens for reasons beyond politics. The Athenians were devoted to beauty in all its manifestations, but especially the beauty of strong young men in their prime — the subject of much of their art. Demetrius, with his athletic physique and exquisite features, inspired a kind of awe as he walked through the city. The other Successors were less well favored, to judge by surviving coin and bust portraits (when these exist), and also much older. Cassander and Lysimachus chose not to disseminate their images at all, which suggests that they did not regard their looks as an asset.

The youthful bloom and military strength of Demetrius combined to produce an impression of godhead in many Greek minds.

Greek legends spoke of a god, Dionysus, who had come from the East into Hellas and whose beauty had inspired mass ecstasy. He had brought freedom to all — that is, liberation from cares and concerns, achieved through ecstatic dancing, revelry, and most of all wine. He used his great power to destroy those who refused to embrace him, as depicted by Euripides in *The Bacchae* (a play performed in the Theater of Dionysus at Athens, during the Dionysia, a festival honoring that god). The play, and the myth on which it was based, highlighted the dual nature of Dionysus — to believers, a source of joy and delight, but a ruinous bane to resisters.

Two decades before the siege of Rhodes, Alexander the Great had linked himself to the legend of Dionysus during his campaign in India, for the god, too, had gone to that distant region. Now it was Demetrius's turn to become a new Dionysus. He too had gone to the East, then returned, bringing liberation to the Hellenic world — in this case, by expelling its garrisons. He too could destroy those who did not accept him. He too could thrill the masses by merely displaying his beauty. Indeed, according to Plutarch, some of those who glimpsed him in the streets and markets of Athens would follow him, magnetized, just to gaze a while longer on those incomparable features.

But Demetrius also resembled Dionysus in less attractive ways, as Athens was soon to learn. When not on a military campaign, he enjoyed wine-soaked binges, sexual escapades, and riotous loose living. To some, his debauches were signs of bravado and dash (and it seems Demetrius capitalized on that notion); to others, they offended decency. No one, however, foresaw how far his libertinism would go, or the depths to which Athens would sink in its willingness to indulge him.

The Besieger arrived in Athens after first chasing Cassander's troops out of central Greece — a decisive win at last, after almost two years of stalemates. A squad of six thousand Macedonian soldiers, deputed to guard the pass of Thermopylae for Cassander, deserted and joined Demetrius's army. The threat Cassander had posed to Athens was instantly dispelled. The city, it seemed, had made a winning bet when it set up two altars to the Savior Gods, meaning, implicitly, Demetrius and his father.

A new altar now joined those other two. At the point where Demetrius entered Athens and stepped down from the running board of his chariot, a shrine was set up to Demetrius *kataibates*, "the Descender." That epithet was usually used of Zeus, who "descended" to earth in the form of a lightning bolt. As the title for a mortal, it marked a new stage in the blurring of earthly and celestial power. Clearly, Stratocles and his crew were on the upswing again, building a cult around Demetrius in order to bolster their own political futures. They passed a measure assigning rewards to whoever held the grandest reception whenever Demetrius entered Athens from elsewhere — the same rewards that were given when effigies of Dionysus and Demeter, two other savior gods, were brought in through the city gates.

Clever demagogues kept finding new ways to cast the Antigonids as Olympians. One involved a magnificent robe, a peplos, brought to the Parthenon every four years as a gift to the goddess Athena in a city-wide ritual called the Panathenaia. The robe depicted Athena and her father, Zeus, in lavish embroidery work. The Assembly now voted that the robe should also depict Antigonus and Demetrius, the newest members of the divine cohort. At the next Panathenaia, a year or two later, the robe would make its highly public debut, spreading out like a sail from the mast of an effigy ship as it was carried toward the Acropolis.

If Demetrius was a god in human form, where was he to dwell? The answer, to the Stratocleans, was clear: in a temple, indeed in the grandest temple of all. No human had ever lodged in the Parthenon, but now the Athenians converted the rear chamber of that sacred structure into Demetrius's personal pied-à-terre. The "front room" of the temple of course belonged to Athena, represented by a magnificent cult statue clad in gold and ivory, but it seemed fitting that these two should share the same roof: Demetrius, swept up in the mood of the moment, and again comparing himself to Dionysus, had begun referring to Athena as his older sister.

The city's love for Demetrius had become an infatuation, but even so, there were some who wanted limits imposed. Their voices were heard after Demetrius intervened in a high-profile court case. The son of the defendant had asked Demetrius to get his father's heavy fine remitted, and Demetrius obliged by giving the boy a letter to bring before the Assembly. The Assembly agreed to cancel the fine, but it also voted that no one should ever again bring a letter from Demetrius before them. It seemed that Athens would not grant *every* license — but when Demetrius grew enraged, the Assembly quickly rescinded the order and punished its supporters. With dissenters thus silenced, the Stratocleans passed a new law, declaring whatever Demetrius did to be righteous and just.

The conundrum of Demetrius was becoming clear to many Athenians: a *god* could not bring freedom and safeguard democracy, for gods were all-powerful and therefore autocrats. Benign dictatorship suited many just fine, but others demurred. Among the latter group was Demochares, nephew and political heir of the great Demosthenes. This man, who had once worn a sword in the Assembly to show his defiance of Macedonian power, regarded Stratocles as a fraud and the pro-Antigonid faction as mere opportunists. When someone called Stratocles "mad" for granting Demetrius total control, Demochares jested bitterly, "He'd be mad not to be mad" — that is, to pass up the gains he could make by toadyism. Demochares was soon banished from Athens for speaking too freely.

Once before, the city had split over a handsome and talented youth. A century earlier Alcibiades had been the darling of many an eye; few dared limit his power. But Alcibiades had let that power go to his head. He had taken part in clandestine soirées where the rites of the gods were mocked; he had even, some said, desecrated the gods' very statues. His enemies played on these signs of autocratic behavior and had the young man indicted and condemned to death in absentia. His backers briefly got him recalled and pardoned, but he died in exile, estranged from the city he very nearly ruled.

If Demetrius ever read the story of Alcibiades, as recorded by Thucydides and Xenophon, he did not absorb its lessons. He too let loose in wild parties that mocked the sanctity of the gods. In his room at the Parthenon, a temple from which even dogs were banned lest they mate in the sacred enclosure, Demetrius held scandalous sex romps with a wide range of partners, both male and female. Chrysis, Demo, and Anticyra were brought to him there, women whom Plutarch describes as *pornai,* common whores, in contrast to the more high-class hetaera, Lamia, who also shared his Parthenon bed. The outrage to sanctity was in a way in his interest: to truly become a god, Demetrius had to go beyond what was licit for humans.

Polygamy was another such boundary. Formerly only the Argead kings of Macedon, Philip and Alexander the Great, had taken multiple wives, as one of the markers of their royal stature. But Ptolemy, it seems, had followed their example even without a crown, and Demetrius, not to be outdone, had taken a second wife, an Athenian named Eurydice, on the occasion of his 307 sojourn in Athens. Now that he had been elevated to kingship (by his father's decree), he had no reason not to add *more* wives, and plenty to gain — alliances and territory — by doing so.

In Epirus, Greece's far north, lived a princess, Deidameia, who had once been betrothed to the young Alexander IV. Demetrius brought her south and contracted his third marriage. The Epirote ties he thereby gained would be crucial if he hoped to challenge Cassander north of Thermopylae. He would have Deidameia's talented brother Pyrrhus as kinsman and ally — or so he might hope.

Though married three times now, and involved in many dalliances, Demetrius remained devoted to Lamia, the greatest love of his life. He annoyed his wives and his other mistresses with his attentions to her and with boasts about her affections. They could not understand his infatuation with a much older woman when younger partners abounded. One hetaera with the suggestive nickname Mania (Madness) was dining with him when a plate of delicacies arrived at the table, a gift from Lamia. Demetrius, jubilant, exclaimed (somewhat callously) to his companion, "You see what Lamia sends me?" Mania replied with bitter point, "My *mother* will send you more gifts than that, if you're willing to sleep with *her*."

For Athenians who disliked or mistrusted Demetrius, his affair with Lamia, and his sex life generally, offered an easy target for slander. A rumor reported by Plutarch, unlikely to be true, held that Demetrius heavily taxed the Athenians, then gave the money to Lamia and other hetaerae to buy scented oil to perfume their skin and hair. The anecdote caricatured the Besieger as a man who put sexual pleasure ahead of the needs of the state. Another, more vicious story told of a beautiful boy, Democles, who died as the result of Demetrius's lust. Democles was determined to stay chaste and so bathed alone rather than in the gymnasia, where older men often seduced younger ones, even boys. Demetrius, who had been stalking Democles, cornered him in his bathing room and would have raped him there, but Democles dove into a vessel of boiling water used to make steam for the bath, instantly killing himself. Such stories, then as now, carried huge political weight; they crystallized in narrative form a people's darkest suspicions about its leaders.

In his introduction to the paired lives of Demetrius and his Roman parallel, Mark Antony, Plutarch says there was a certain "savagery" in Demetrius's pursuit of pleasure, and alludes specifically to the story of Democles. In episodes like this, Plutarch claims, Demetrius compares poorly with Antony, who harmed only himself, not others, by his addiction to pleasure. Both men, says Plutarch, inclined toward hubris — not only arrogant pride, but a selfish violence coming from it — when they were flush with success, and Demetrius in Athens in 304 was certainly riding high. It is not unlikely that with Stratocles giving him license to do as he pleased, he became predatory, though the Democles story reads more like a dark fantasy.

Lamia climbed high enough in stature to have a lore of her own, apart from her ties to Demetrius. Plutarch retells a story that demonstrates her wit and her solidarity with her fellow hetaerae, in this case an Egyptian woman named Thonis. It seems a wealthy man was besotted with Thonis and offered her a large sum of money for sex. But before consummation took place, the man had a wet dream involving Thonis, which quenched his desire. Thonis brought suit claiming that after sleeping with her in the dream he owed her the promised fee. A judge ruled that the man had to bring the money and move it around in his hand, and Thonis could take hold of its shadow, for dreams, the judge reasoned, are like the shadows of life. Lamia enters the tale as its commentator: she claimed, Plutarch tells us, that Thonis was cheated, since shadows of money did not give *her* satisfaction, but clearly the young man's dream had satisfied *him*.

Demetrius's attachment to Lamia attained a kind of salacious fame, as seen in a fictional love letter composed by Alciphron, a Greek writer of uncertain date. In the letter, contained in a set of epistles ascribed to famous hetaerae, Lamia addresses Demetrius in affectionate, sometimes worshipful tones, exalting his magnificence and control. She worries that he will become bored with her because she cannot use the usual tricks by which hetaerae keep men on the hook, delaying fulfillment with ruses and made-up tasks; she's too fond of him to play games. Yet Demetrius seems to be hooked all the same, to judge by her descriptions of his passionate kisses. She ends by promising him a lavish dinner at the upcoming festival of Aphrodite—as potent an occasion for lovers, in the Greek world, as our Saint Valentine's Day.

Perhaps this promised banquet is the same one Plutarch refers to, in less positive tones, in his *Demetrius*. He says that Lamia, no doubt leveraging her lover's authority, squeezed money from the Athenians to pay for the meal. The resulting feast was so lavish, and required so many extortions, that one wag dubbed Lamia "a veritable helepolis," a city-sacker like the enormous siege towers Demetrius built on Cyprus and Rhodes.

Even Demetrius's officers found amusement in their leader's grand passion for this demimondaine. A team of his envoys, writes Plutarch, was dispatched to the court of Lysimachus in Thrace, where they were regaled with stories from the great days of Alexander. Lysimachus one day revealed some scars on his shoulders and legs and recounted a time when Alexander, incensed by some slight, had shut him in a cage with a rampaging lion. The envoys laughed and declared that Demetrius also had scars from a fearsome wild beast—the marks that passionate Lamia left on his neck.

We do not know how long the love affair lasted or how it ended; perhaps it went on until Lamia's death, about which we have no record. She bore Demetrius a daughter, and since she was older than he, and therefore old for childbearing, it has been surmised that she died in childbirth. We also do not know what became of the daughter, to whom Demetrius, in a move that was either bizarrely tone-deaf or out-and-out cruel, gave the name Phila, after his long-suffering, aristocratic first wife.

Departing from Athens and his Parthenon orgies, Demetrius swept through the Peloponnese with his army, purging it of Cassander's garrisons. One by one these fortresses fell to the famous siege weapons, some hauled across land, others brought to bear by sea against coastal cities. In Sicyon the garrison surrendered as soon as the machines rolled into place, and the soldiers were given leave to depart for Ptolemy's Egypt. To prevent the city being retaken, Demetrius reshaped it for better defense, moving the population to higher ground and demolishing low-lying neighborhoods. This newly organized state was named Demetrias (though the name did not stick; the place soon became Sicyon once again).

Not all of Cassander's garrison troops were so easily dealt with. The commander of a fort at Orchomenus not only refused to surrender but hurled taunts at Demetrius from atop the city walls. The Besieger had not thus far indulged in punitive rage, but now, evidently, his ego asserted itself, along with the need to terrorize other resisters. Upon taking the city, Diodorus reports, he had the commander crucified at the town gates, along with some eighty of the man's loyalists. The message was clearly received by Cassander's less stalwart soldiers, for two thousand of them switched sides and joined with Demetrius, while others surrendered or fled.

The "liberation" of Greece (as some saw it) was nearly complete by the summer of 303. Athenians were ecstatic. They had begun to call Demetrius not only soter but *megas,* "Great," and commissioned a new statue of him, seated on horseback, to be set up in the Agora beside that of personified Democracy. Athenian troops who fought in the Peloponnesian campaign sent home glowing reports of its speed and effectiveness. The Stratocles faction in the Assembly, the sponsors of the apotheosis program, grew ever more influential. But then a letter arrived and was read aloud to that body that put Stratocles in a difficult spot.

Demetrius wrote that on his return to Athens, he wanted to be initiated into the Mystery cult at Eleusis, and that this must be done and concluded in very short order. Athenians were proud and protective of this cult, as seen in the fact that its rites were never disclosed or recorded (giving rise to the meaning of our word "mystery"). Its lengthy initiation process began in the month called Anthesterion (in early spring), continued in Boedromion (in the fall), and ended with a transformational rite — some sort of transcendent vision — that took place more than a year after the first two stages. At the time Demetrius wrote, the month of Anthesterion had just passed. He would normally need to wait a year to even begin the process, then take another year and a half to complete it — an eon, in the frenzied career of the Besieger.

Religious laws were hard for Athens to bend, since doing so offended the gods, but if a *god* wanted them bent, what was the Assembly to do? Stratocles devised a solution: The current month, in mid-spring, could be renamed Anthesterion, allowing Demetrius to start his initiation; then the same month could immediately be renamed Boedromion, so he could move to the second stage. The yearlong interval before the final rite could simply be ignored. A ripple of dissent went through the Assembly, but the measures were passed nonetheless. A new Anthesterion was proclaimed, and Demetrius started his initiation; he concluded it promptly in a new Boedromion. Again Demetrius had shown his greater-than-human status, for, at his behest, time itself had been made to speed up.

He could not, however, command the elements. The wind, ever his bane when he commanded ships on the seas, at last, in 302, gave a rebuke to the movement that had divinized him.

That was a year of the quadrennial Panathenaia, when Athena's new robe, now embroidered with images of Demetrius and his father, made its debut. As custom dictated, it was spread like a sail on a miniature ship, a kind of parade float, that was brought up the Sacred Way toward the Acropolis. As all the city looked on, a sudden whirlwind struck the "sail" from behind and tore it to tatters.

Another such weather anomaly attended the Dionysia, the festival at which Dionysus was ritually brought into Athens. The springtime fest in 302 brought a killing frost that withered the shoots just starting to sprout in the fields. Athenians could look forward to a slim harvest and the threat of a famine — unless of course their savior god stepped into the breach, with life-giving shipments of grain.

Decades later, when it was safe to do so, the comic playwright Philippides, who had evidently faced public scorn for some of his plays, allowed one of his characters to comment on Demetrius's sojourn in Athens. The passage was quoted later by Plutarch:

He telescoped the year into one month,

He turned the Acropolis into a boarding house

And made virgin Athena share digs with courtesans.

Demetrius the Descender

On his account the vines were withered by frost;
Because of his impiety, the robe was rent in the middle,
Since he made the honors of gods apply to mortal men.
It's this that destroys a society — *not my comedies!*

CHAPTER ELEVEN

The War of the Five Armies

The Antigonid father-son team controlled two continents now, with the son victorious in Greece and the father established in Asia. Their prospects of reattaching the empire of Alexander and bringing unified rule to a fragmented world seemed markedly improved by 302. But they had not as yet eliminated a single obstacle to that goal. Cassander was beaten in Greece but firmly ensconced in Macedon; Lysimachus was unchallenged in Thrace, Seleucus in Babylon; and Ptolemy now considered Egypt spear-won land, successfully defended against an invasion and therefore incontestably *his*. All four of these rivals wore crowns. The game of global dominion was still a five-way free-for-all.

Those in the lead, Demetrius and his father, as always hoped to knock others out of the game, starting this time with Cassander, now greatly weakened in Europe. But the targeted player, as always, sought the help of the other non-leaders, who naturally feared they would be next in line if one of their number fell. Cassander first approached Lysimachus, his nearest neighbor; then the two of them enlisted Seleucus and Ptolemy. In no time, the old anti-

Antigonid league was re-formed. It moved into action in Europe and Asia at once, hoping to force a fight on two fronts that a single enemy, even a father-son team, could not withstand.

A new round of Diadoch warfare was under way, more complex and dynamic than any previous stage. This time all the contestants were on the march at once, arcing and wheeling across the continents, seeking a final showdown. It was truly a world war, and the world itself seemed to be its ultimate prize.

For the anti-Antigonid axis, much depended on matters of timing and troop allotment. Cassander kept enough troops to pin Demetrius down in northern Greece, then gave the rest, including his senior general Prepelaus, to Lysimachus, who was preparing to cross into Asia. The goal was to bring Antigonus to battle in Anatolia before he could be joined there by his son. So Cassander went on the attack in Thessaly, drawing Demetrius into the field, while Lysimachus and Prepelaus crossed the Hellespont and began eating away at Antigonid holdings in Asia. From the south and east, Ptolemy and Seleucus made their way toward Lysimachus, hoping to rendezvous with him and later (if he arrived) Cassander, in a four-way pincer movement.

Demetrius as yet perceived little of this grand plan, though he knew that Lysimachus had gone into Asia. Demetrius had a huge army by this time, including almost fifty thousand heavy infantry; he could have sent nearly half to his father's aid and still matched Cassander's numbers. But he lived by the rule that bigger is better, so he kept his huge aggregate force intact as he marched into Thessaly, sending only a small squad across the Aegean to deal with Lysimachus and Prepelaus. Those generals were making good progress as they moved down the Anatolian coast, taking cities, harbors, and a treasury stuffed with coin away from the Antigonid cause.

Had he known how great a danger he and his father faced,

Demetrius might have wasted no time in bringing Cassander to battle, but he did not press his numerical advantage. His thinking is hard to discern at this point, since Plutarch, who gives us our best access into his mind, passes over this Thessalian campaign without a word. We know that Demetrius made a few gains, but when he and Cassander approached the same plain and encamped on opposite ends, he did not take steps that would have brought on a showdown. Both armies remained in their camps for weeks, with neither forcing the issue. Meanwhile reports kept arriving about the progress of Lysimachus and Prepelaus in Anatolia.

The same reports reached Antigonus in Syria, in his newly built capital city on the Orontes River, Antigoneia. One-Eye had prepared an arts and sports festival there to commemorate the city's foundation in good Hellenic style. He was past eighty now, overweight and slow, but he went into rapid motion when he heard that his Anatolian cities were falling one by one. He canceled the festival before it had even begun, collected his army, and set out on a march of more than five hundred miles. He stopped en route at Cyinda, a fort in Cilicia, and drew out funds from the treasury to give his troops three months' pay in advance; he did not want his rivals luring defectors away, as they had in the past.

Ptolemy and Seleucus were also on the march, moving along their separate routes to link up with Lysimachus. Antigonus knew they were coming, for envoys and scouts were flying about from one camp to another. Taking advantage of this network, Antigonus tried a ruse that became famous—perhaps undeservedly—as a use of disinformation. If the story is true, he sent his own messengers, disguised as those of his foes, to Ptolemy's camp. These undercover agents found Ptolemy besieging Sidon and reported, falsely, that Antigonus had won a battle in Asia and was on his way south for another invasion of Egypt. Perhaps Ptolemy believed this, or perhaps he wanted a pretext to go back home, or perhaps — the most likely scenario — he never received any envoys at all, but pretended he had to create that pretext. Whatever the case, Ptolemy promptly reversed his steps and returned to the Nile, leaving Sidon still in Antigonid hands. His departure would later cause conflict within his alliance.

Meanwhile, Seleucus was on his way west, but making slow progress with his elephant herd. Lysimachus, with too few troops to fight One-Eye on his own, needed to stall until Seleucus arrived. He camped in a strong position and fortified his perimeter, knowing Antigonus would try to bring him to battle. Indeed, One-Eye was soon on the scene with his army arrayed for a fight, but Lysimachus did not come forth. Antigonus used his numbers to wall off the camp and deprive it of food; starvation could force a battle he knew he would win. But Lysimachus broke camp in the dead of night, found an unguarded route, and marched off to a new locale where his army could live off the land. There he again built a fortified camp and awaited Seleucus.

Both Demetrius and Antigonus must have by now understood, from their different perspectives, the scale and cunning of the campaign against them. But for some reason Demetrius stayed where he was, in Thessaly, with his huge aggregation of largely inactive troops. Perhaps he feared to lose Athens, and therefore the rest of Greece, unless he destroyed Cassander once and for all; or perhaps his imperious father insisted on fighting alone, confident in his superior numbers and skill. Both men regarded Lysimachus with contempt; Demetrius liked to hear him called a *gazophylax*, a treasury guard, in a game of insult toasts that was played at his court. The point of the jibe may have been that such guards in Asian lands were frequently eunuchs. Lysimachus took the remark very ill when others reported it to him. He lashed out at Demetrius with a low blow, deriding his beloved Lamia as a common prostitute.

With an energy remarkable in a man his age, Antigonus marched to Lysimachus's new encampment, built a ring of forts to surround it, and sent for siege weapons, intending to take it by storm. He saw clearly now that he must eliminate one of his two nearest foes before they joined forces. He had Lysimachus in a choke hold—or so it seemed—but Lysimachus, too, felt the urgency of his position. He managed yet again to find a gap in One-Eye's siege cordon and slipped from the trap. Once more he marched off in the night, and once more Antigonus blew the trumpets at dawn and set off in pursuit.

By now it was early winter, the rainy season in Mediterranean lands. Lysimachus followed a route that took him across high ground, but Antigonus stayed on the plains, keeping pace with his foe. Then the rains fell in torrents. The lowlands turned into a sea of mud, through which the Antigonid army had to struggle. Pack animals sometimes sank so deep they could not be extracted, and even some soldiers were claimed by the mud, according to Diodorus. On his upland route, Lysimachus had easier going. Finally, Antigonus had no choice; he called a halt and gave up the pursuit. Then he sent for his son.

Demetrius was still holding Cassander at bay when the summons came from his father, telling him to negotiate a stand-down and bring his army to Asia without delay. As he had done at Babylon and Rhodes, he dropped his campaign at his father's request, leaving his own job undone. He and Cassander signed a pact of mutual disengagement, with the proviso that Antigonus had to approve its terms before they could take effect. That clause, as Demetrius knew, would scuttle the pact, for his father would never accept it. In any case he only needed the treaty as cover for his withdrawal. He could not let the Greeks think that his retreat came from weakness; he needed to keep them under his thumb while he went into Asia.

As the winter of 302–301 closed in, Demetrius brought his army across the Hellespont, which he still controlled, to join up with his father. Cassander again took possession of Thessaly, then dispatched more troops—another twelve thousand soldiers and five hundred horsemen, under command of his brother Pleistarchus—to reinforce his ally Lysimachus. Forced to cross by way of the Black Sea instead of the Hellespont, this force was beset by storms and enemy ships, and only a third arrived on the Asian shore. The flagship was wrecked in mid-crossing, and Pleistarchus barely survived, washing up half-dead on the beach. But soon he recovered and made his way with a few thousand men toward the Lysimachan camp.

Seleucus continued his westward trek from Babylon, accompanied by his lumbering elephant herd. Five armies were set to converge in Anatolia—those of Seleucus, Pleistarchus, and Lysimachus, facing those of Demetrius and his father. Such a huge showdown could not be anything but decisive. When the rains ended, the question of Antigonid power, and the bridging of Europe and Asia, would at last be resolved.

That winter's reunion of Demetrius and Antigonus must have been a meaningful one, since both knew it might be their last. Over the course of two decades they had rarely fought, or lived, together, and at this point it had been years since they had seen each other. Their past greetings were known for warmth, even exuberance. On one occasion the young man, returning from a journey abroad, had given his father a kiss that seemed almost amorous. "My son, you seem like you're kissing Lamia!" Antigonus had joked. But this time there was little occasion for levity.

As the winter dragged on, nerves had worn thin, as well as supplies. Lysimachus seems to have run short of money or provisions or both; a contingent of his troops, two thousand Autiaratae from the Balkans and eight hundred members of Anatolian tribes, deserted to Antigonus, complaining of missing pay. One-Eye, with fuller coffers, made good their arrears and rewarded them with gifts. Such defections delivered a blow to his foe's morale, as Antigonus knew; he had suffered the same problem himself on his invasion of Egypt, and had felt the need to use torture to stop the erosion. Lysimachus, fearing that more Autiaratae would leave him, resorted to an even more desperate cruelty: he lured five thousand onto open ground, on the pretext of doling out rations, then slaughtered them where they stood. Better to lose auxiliaries in this way than have them decamp to his foes.

For Seleucus, who by now had arrived in the region, the problem of supplies pressed especially hard, for he had hundreds of elephants to feed. He'd acquired a herd of five hundred the previous year by way of his treaty with Chandragupta Maurya, relinquishing his claims on the East in exchange for those beasts, heavy weapons for war on Antigonus. Now he had brought them across half of Asia, confirming the mocking title awarded him at the Antigonid court: *elephantarch*, a glorified zookeeper. How well he maintained them is hard to say, but it seems that their number by now had shrunk by nearly a hundred.

Lysimachus and Seleucus now drew close enough to join forces, a juncture that the Antigonids would have done well to prevent. Why they failed to do so is uncertain, but Antigonus was perhaps, at this early stage, too sure of himself. Plutarch reports his remark that he needed only a single stone and a shout to scatter his aggregate foes as easily as if they were a flock of birds feeding on grain. That was his usual manner when battle was near: boastfulness, bluster, and braggadocio, signals to all those around that he did not feel fear.

But on the eve of the clash, this big-talking man became eerily quiet and thoughtful, and was seen in hushed conversations with Demetrius in his tent. Historians would give a lot to know what was said in those meetings. The father-son team was nearing a moment of truth; the fate of much of the world depended on their collaboration. As usual Demetrius was to play the attack role, commanding the heavy-armed cavalry wing that would charge from the right. Antigonus would hang back with the infantry phalanx and watch for the cavalry charge to disrupt the enemy's lines. He needed his son to keep a cool head and maintain good formation, but Demetrius had not led a cavalry charge in quite a long time.

How much confidence did Demetrius inspire? He had failed to win in Egypt, at Rhodes, and most recently in Thessaly when facing Cassander. Plutarch reports that at this crucial moment, Antigonus presented him to an army assembly and proclaimed him the "successor" to his realm—a point that should not have needed proclaiming. Did One-Eye perceive in his men a lack of faith in his son? Had Demetrius gained the adoration of Athens, a city of fanciful artists and scheming politicians, but not the loyalty of veteran soldiers—toughened, no-nonsense men who measured weakness and strength with expert eyes?

Demetrius himself had misgivings about the coming battle, if we trust a report of his dreams in the days just before it. According to Plutarch, he dreamed that Alexander appeared before him in brilliant armor and gear, and asked what password Demetrius and his father would use in the coming fight. Such passwords, meant to distinguish friend from foe, were typically formed by pairing the names of two gods, but in past years they had often included the name Alexander in place of one deity's name. In a battle two decades before this, one side had used "Athena and Alexander" as its password, the other "Alexander and Demeter." But in the dream, Demetrius told Alexander his password would be "Zeus and Victory." "Then I'll go and join your opponents," Alexander replied, dismayed at being omitted. "*They* will be sure to receive me."

Of all the dreams Plutarch records in his *Parallel Lives* — his way of exploring his subjects' interior lives — this one is perhaps the most layered and revealing. From the time of his first combat command at age eighteen, Demetrius had sought to embody the spirit of Alexander, the most potent ghost the world had ever known. He alone, of all the Successors, possessed the youthfulness, vigor, and beauty that could capture imaginations as Alexander's had done. But in his key tests, he had failed to achieve Alexandrian triumphs, or indeed many triumphs at all. Now he was going forth to the greatest test yet with a sense of inadequacy.

Antigonus too had a warning of what lay ahead, on the very morning of battle. As he stepped from his tent to join his infantry phalanx, he tripped and fell flat on his face. For an overweight man in his eighties, the fall was no doubt painful, perhaps injurious, but also a very bad omen. One-Eye rose from the ground with his hands outstretched in prayer to the gods. He asked them to grant him either victory in the coming fight or else, in defeat, a death without pain. He was to be given neither.

The Battle of Ipsus brought together a greater mass of armed force than any other clash in Greek history. Each side had about eighty thousand troops in the field, according to Plutarch (our only source for these numbers). Antigonus and Demetrius had a slightly lower proportion of cavalry, a distinct disadvantage, but theirs were heavy-armed Companions, more lethal than the light horse of Lysimachus and Seleucus. Armored horsemen had won every battle for Alexander the Great, and at Ipsus they seemed likely to tilt the contest in the Antigonids' favor. They were to be led by Demetrius on the right wing, the place from which Alexander had also led them.

To meet this all-too-predictable charge, Seleucus's oldest son, Antiochus, now in his early twenties, led a cavalry squad on the left of the Lysimachan line. Seleucus himself held the right wing, with a squad of mounted archers and javelin men. These light-armed horsemen could not break apart a well-ordered phalanx, but they could soften it up with barrages of missiles, or else, if things went well elsewhere, pursue fleeing men and cut them down from behind. In the center, leading the infantry, stood Lysimachus, facing Antigonus, similarly positioned. Behind each of these aging warlords, two massive walls of foot soldiers, each stretching out more than a mile, bristled with eighteen-foot spears, waiting to tweeze at one another to pry open a fatal gap.

Demetrius had derided Seleucus as an elephant keeper, but in fact *both* sides were deploying the elephant weapon at Ipsus. These beasts not only functioned as tanks when driven toward phalanx lines; they also deflected cavalry charges, for horses were terrified of them. Antigonus stationed some seventy-five in front of his lines, where they could fulfill both functions. Seleucus had with him a much larger herd; he posted enough at *his* front to match those of Antigonus, and kept all the rest—three hundred or so—in the rear. In the plan he had crafted to deal with Demetrius, these rear-guard beasts had a critical role to play.

The battle began, as all had foreknown, with a charge by Demetrius and his heavy-armed horsemen. Thousands of these thundered across the plain and attacked their opposite numbers, led by

Antiochus. The lighter-armed horsemen engaged, then fell back in retreat, perhaps by design. Demetrius did what his foes had anticipated: he urged his cavalry forward in pursuit. He could finish Antiochus off, he supposed, then return to attack his enemy's phalanx from rear and from side — a time-worn and reliable strategy.

But he'd fallen into a trap. As he moved farther off in pursuit, Seleucus brought his rear-guard elephants into a screen formation. When Demetrius doubled back, he found that his path was blocked.

Plutarch, our best source for this battle, here shifts his gaze from Demetrius to his father. Antigonus, not yet engaged with the foe, stood amid the infantry phalanx and watched for his son's return from pursuit. Seleucus was leading his mounted archers against this phalanx, riding around to its side and rear, from where they could launch their spears and arrows. Unharassed by Companion horsemen — for these were far from the field — Seleucus could rain down darts on his foe at will, or else mount a charge to their rear with even more lethal effect. Lysimachus's phalanx meanwhile advanced to attack from the front.

Antigonus's infantrymen, unprotected by cavalry, were now at Seleucus's mercy and they knew it. Many abandoned their leader, laying down arms or changing sides before they had even engaged with the opposite phalanx. As his line ebbed away, Antigonus stood his ground with a cadre of loyal supporters. One of them warned that his foes had him in their sights; "Who else should they target?" he asked, with characteristic sangfroid. He still expected his son to come galloping to his rescue. That was what Alexander had done, in nearly the same situation, to save Parmenio, his senior commander, at the Battle of Gaugamela.

But as the phalanx collapsed, no rescue appeared. To the last, Antigonus watched for the dust cloud raised by returning horsemen. Then a hail of javelins came whistling out of the sky, and Antigonus fell dead where he stood.

A single loyal attendant, Thorax of Larissa, stayed by the corpse to protect it from being trampled. The others made haste to flee, for the battle was lost.

Somewhere behind the elephant screen, unobserved by our sources, an agonized Demetrius sought a way out of his trap, aware that he was letting his father down as no son ever had, and losing most of his empire.

CHAPTER TWELVE

Lord of the Isles

With his intact but defeated cavalry corps, Demetrius dashed for the port of Ephesus, more than two hundred miles to the west of the Ipsus battlefield. His foes were either too slow or too tired to pursue him. He had five thousand horsemen with him when he arrived at Ephesus and four thousand infantrymen, the latter probably garrison forces collected along the way. There was no point any longer in keeping men in his Anatolian forts; his Asian holdings were forfeit.

There was little time to grieve for his father's death or regret having partially caused it. He had to marshal his resources and show the world he was not a beaten man. His strength lay in his navy and in the ports and harbors he still controlled throughout the eastern Mediterranean, places like Ephesus, Sidon, Tyre, and the cities of Cyprus. In Europe he had Corinth in his control, and also Athens, or so he might think, but he had not yet learned how changeable Athens could be.

He needed money to pay for his ships and their crews. The Ephesians were certain he intended to plunder their Temple of

Artemis, a magnificent structure, one of the Seven Wonders of the World, where rich dedications were housed. Instead, Demetrius boarded ship and sailed to Cilicia, off to the east, to collect funds from his palace and evacuate his wife Phila, his children by her, and his mother, Stratonice. Cilicia now belonged to Cassander's brother Pleistarchus as part of the division of spoils among the victors of Ipsus; Lysimachus received large parts of Anatolia, while the rest of that region and Mesopotamia went to Seleucus. Syria was claimed by both Seleucus and Ptolemy, the grounds for future disputes between these two.

Before Pleistarchus arrived at Cilicia to claim his new lands, Demetrius relocated his family to Cyprus, which now became his principal base. The island had good dockyards, harbors, and ship sheds, as well as a ready supply of silver, plus a mint with which to strike coin. Demetrius began issuing currency from this mint and from Ephesus too, proclaiming to the world his new naval posture. These coins depicted a grandly naked Poseidon holding a trident and, on the reverse, a figure of Nike, goddess of victory, on the prow of a warship. The inscription proclaimed the coin that "of King Demetrius," for king he remained, though monarch now of a diffuse realm that spanned hundreds of miles of salt water and also included parts of "free" Greece.

Other coins that appeared at this time depicted Demetrius himself with small horns on his head that signified godhead. This followed the precedent set by Ptolemy, who had already begun stamping his own face on coins—the first Western ruler to do so. Demetrius went him one better by adorning his coin portrait with attributes of a god (probably Poseidon or Dionysus). Such measures were part of the new age to come, an age in which political power would merge with divinity.

At Athens, the leaders who'd honored Demetrius as a god were deeply shaken by his stunning defeat. Stratocles and his faction were overthrown in the Assembly; new orators took the reins there and passed a measure forbidding the city to admit any "kings." This was cleverly phrased in general terms but clearly targeted Demetrius alone. Word of the banishment reached Demetrius in the Cycladic Islands, a stopping point on his way toward mainland Greece. Envoys told him that his most recent wife, Deidameia, and his royal effects had been sent to Megara to prevent him from entering Athens to gather them up. The news enraged Demetrius, but he accepted the ban — for the time being. He asked that his ships in Piraeus, including his giant thirteener, be restored to his control, and the Athenians agreed.

Among Demetrius's retinue was Deidameia's brother, a teenager named Pyrrhus, who was heir to the throne of Epirus in northern Greece. Exiled as a baby when a collateral branch of his family seized power, he was briefly restored to the throne as a child, then exiled again. He then joined the retinue of Demetrius, fought with distinction at Ipsus, and stayed loyal to the Antigonid house in retreat. Now he became the Besieger's righthand man, entrusted to shore up positions in Greece. This talented, spirited youth was soon to join the great game of global dominion as yet another contestant, and to cut a swath through his troubled era almost as large as that of Demetrius.

Still in need of more cash, Demetrius made sea raids on the Thracian coast, Lysimachan territory. His success showed what control of the sea might achieve and also inflicted some measure of revenge. He met with no great opposition, for it seemed that the old alliance against him, victorious at Ipsus, was showing its fault lines. Neither Seleucus nor Ptolemy cared much to help Lysimachus — and indeed, those two were at odds, contesting a valuable portion of Syria. Ptolemy claimed these lands as part of the spoils of the Ipsus war, having come a ways north to aid the alliance's cause. But Seleucus maintained that when Ptolemy turned south and abandoned that cause, not joining the crucial battle, he forfeited his rights to any spoils. The two came near to blows when Seleucus appeared in Syria with his army; in the end he backed off but declared in threatening terms that the matter had not been settled.

Little by little, this festering dispute began to turn the global contest in a new direction, aiding immensely the reeling Demetrius.

Ptolemy, it seems, feared Seleucus as much as he once feared Antigonus, in part because of those plentiful elephants. He owned only a few of the beasts himself and could not get more, for he had not begun trapping and training the African species, as his descendants would later do. Connection to the Far East gave Seleucus sole access to this important weapon. So Ptolemy reached out to Lysimachus and struck an exclusive alliance, sending one of his daughters, Arsinoe, to Thrace to become his wife.

Seleucus observed this marital power play and decided to try a similar gambit himself. He was already wed to a remarkable Iranian woman, Apama; she was the mother of Antiochus, the son who played such a vital role at the Battle of Ipsus. But polygamy was now fair game among the Successors, and besides, as Plutarch reports, Seleucus considered his vast territory "enough for more heirs than just one." His position in western Asia would be greatly strengthened if he had the help of a navy—and Demetrius had such a navy. So he sent to Demetrius a request to wed Stratonice, the Besieger's daughter by Phila, a girl now perhaps in her mid-teens.

For the principal victor of Ipsus, whose battle plan had led to the death by spear of Antigonus One-Eye, to propose to marry into a house he had nearly destroyed, and for Demetrius to accept that proposal—as he instantly did—gives good insight into the strange, Cosa Nostra–like world of the Successors. Expedience and advantage governed all their relations; no hatred was ever permanent, and no amity either. Their most reliable bonds were those of kinship and marriage, forged when they swapped their daughters and sisters for allied support. But even those bonds might fail when power and land were at stake.

Demetrius, delighted at his sudden reversal of fortune, set out with his entire fleet for the Levantine coast, stopping at Cyprus to pick up the bride and her mother. His huge flotilla was not only a matter of pageantry. Demetrius felt his stature rising, bringing new hope that the losses of Ipsus — apart from the death of his father — could soon be repaired. Losing Cilicia to Pleistarchus, his own brother-in-law, grieved him sorely, but with the naval power he still possessed he hoped for a measure of payback. On his way to the meeting with Seleucus he raided Cilician coastal towns and purloined a large sum of money from the Cynda treasury. As he anticipated, no one, including Pleistarchus, dared challenge his fleet.

With his coffers replenished, Demetrius sailed on to Rhossus, on the Syrian coast, and rendezvoused with Seleucus and his land army. As far as is known this was the first meeting between Demetrius, now in his mid-thirties, and Seleucus, some twenty years older; they had fought one another for years but never come face to face. Ceremonies and feasts were held to commemorate the occasion, some on Demetrius's enormous flagship — the thirteener he got back from Athens — some in Seleucus's sumptuous tent on land. The two men made a display of their concord, dispensing with bodyguards to show they did not fear one another. The world had to see that their bonding was real; envoys were sent to proclaim it to Greeks farther west. At some point amid these festivities the wedding took place, and Seleucus marched off with his bride to his new capital, Antiocheia.

Demetrius had learned by now what Athens had discovered in the days of Pericles: the special nature of sea power. To control the sea required not only money and oarsmen but timber for ships (not easy to come by), as well as the expertise of shipbuilders. These resources could put a huge gap between haves and have-nots. With his keen technological mind, Demetrius had made advances in naval warfare that far outpaced his rivals, building enormous ships and mounting artillery weapons on their decks. His fleet made him a *nesiarch,* lord of the isles—the very title his court had once given to Agathocles, a Sicilian tyrant, when devising mocking toasts to lampoon other dynasts. The fleet also made him invaluable to Seleucus, a counterpart on the sea to Seleucus's elephant strength on land.

Bolstered by this new partnership, Demetrius returned to Cilicia from Rhossus and made a much bolder attack. He landed troops in force and seized forts and strongholds, chasing Pleistarchus back to Macedon. After less than two years in exile, he meant to reestablish himself in his former seat. His rivals took note with alarm, especially Cassander, who now heard his brother's outraged account of "the common enemy." Demetrius sent Phila—now acting as ambassador and peacemaker, an unusual role for a woman—to Macedon to settle her two brothers down and stop them from doing anything rash in Asia.

Ptolemy too felt the danger implied by these moves in Cilicia. The trees of the Amanus Mountains in the eastern part of the region furnished excellent shipbuilding timber, and Tyre and Sidon, the best ports on the Levantine coast, still belonged to Demetrius. His adversary could do him much harm; with Seleucus at his side, the Besieger might invade Egypt again, and succeed where he had failed before, at the mouths of the Nile. But Seleucus too was now apparently wary of the man he called father-in-law (though Demetrius was twenty years his junior). With control of Cilicia, the man was a bit too close for his liking, and a bit too strong as well, with so many vessels and ports.

So Seleucus and Ptolemy were at odds over Syria, and both men mistrusted Demetrius, who might give either the means to take down the other. The triangle of suspicion among these three kings called for a three-way negotiation. Seleucus orchestrated the diplomacy in an effort to bring Demetrius and Ptolemy closer together. In a parley from which few records survive — perhaps conducted by emissaries — the three greatest powers of the eastern Mediterranean struggled toward an accord.

Ultimately it was agreed that to prevent hostilities, Demetrius would marry *again* and become Ptolemy's son-in-law. A match was arranged between Demetrius and Ptolemaïs, one of Ptolemy's five daughters (also Demetrius's niece by marriage, since her mother was Phila's sister). In a further move toward détente, Demetrius sent two members of his family, the trusty Pyrrhus and his own son by Deidameia, a boy then perhaps five years old, to live at Ptolemy's court as pledges of good faith. It seemed for a time that the worst of the Successor enmities — the grudge match between Ptolemy and Demetrius stretching back two decades — had come to an end.

Somehow, though, the wedding, and the rapprochement, failed to take place, and low-level warfare resumed. Demetrius struck inland from Tyre and raided Samaria, in Ptolemy's Syrian territory, land also claimed by Seleucus. By doing so he antagonized both men, quite possibly by intent. Seleucus by now had a daughter by Stratonice, Demetrius's first grandchild, and the Besieger may have been testing how far this new bond could be stretched. Seleucus only partially obliged him. He asked his father-in-law to cede control of Cilicia, but in deference to family ties offered to compensate him for the loss.

Demetrius refused this request. Seleucus became angry and increased his demands: he wanted Tyre and Sidon as well, this time without any offer of recompense. Demetrius stood his ground, declaring he would rather lose ten thousand Ipsuses than "hire" Seleucus as a son-in-law (that is, surrender possessions to preserve kinship bonds). Then he strengthened the garrisons, showing he was prepared to fight to keep what he had. His relations with Seleucus were back on a hostile footing, despite the days they had spent together without bodyguards, despite the merry feasting on board Demetrius's thirteener.

Four years after Ipsus, the world had learned that Demetrius had *not* been knocked out of the contest for empire. His spirit and drive were as ardent as ever, as his mistrustful rivals — even Seleucus, his new son-in-law — were keenly aware. He was still a king, after all, though he had no contiguous realm to reign over. The quest for such a realm would take him on the next leg of his zigzag journey and return him to Greece.

CHAPTER THIRTEEN

In Search of a Kingdom

In 296 Demetrius and his magnificent fleet crossed the Aegean again, headed for mainland Greece. Two developments there had drawn the Besieger's attention. In Macedon, on the legacy throne of Alexander's empire, a dynastic crisis was taking shape: Cassander had died the previous year of disease, and his sickly eldest son had followed him to the grave a few months later. The two remaining heirs were both rather young for the throne and, inevitably, at odds with each other. Also, in central Greece, Athens had fallen under the rule of a despot, a warlord named Lachares, and was in a miserable state, riven by factionalism and increasingly short of food.

Demetrius had been barred from Athens by decree of the Assembly, but before that exile he had also been divinized by the same body. He had seen how volatile the Athenian democracy was, how easily Athenians could change their views, and their political leadership, to adapt to circumstances. Now the city was under the thumb of a tyrant, which gave Demetrius the chance to play the liberator once again. And if he could win back Athens — the beacon of Greece, as his father had thought, projecting the image it saw to the rest of the Hellenized world — he might go much farther, perhaps even as far as Macedon, the place of his birth.

But on his arrival in Greece, the winds once again played him false. As he cruised off the coast near Athens, barred from Piraeus by Assembly decree, a great storm arose and wrecked a number of his vessels. Undeterred, he sent for replacements from Cyprus, draining his eastern resources to support his campaign in the West. His enemies, ever alert for signs of weakness, took note of that shift. Seleucus soon took control of Cilicia, and Lysimachus led a campaign down the Ionian coast, taking over the crucial port of Ephesus. Ptolemy made an even bolder move, capturing Sidon and Tyre at last and launching an attack against Cyprus, the island Demetrius had long ago taken from him.

Demetrius could not defend his Asian positions while committing so many resources to Europe. He must have guessed that he would lose Cilicia, perhaps Sidon and Tyre as well, by withdrawing his ships from the East, but no doubt he thought Cyprus secure; he had left his whole family there. Besides, with the manpower and money that control of Hellas could bring him, he must have assumed he could cross the Aegean again and make good any losses on the eastern side. He could use Europe as a staging ground for an invasion of Asia, just as Alexander the Great had done with such astonishing success.

While awaiting the replacement fleet from Cyprus, Demetrius campaigned by land in the Peloponnese. Cassander had reestablished himself there before his death, and some cities remained loyal to his heirs, the quarreling joint kings of Macedon. The going was often rough. While besieging Messene, a city with stout stone walls, Demetrius was hit by a catapult bolt that penetrated his jaw and went into his mouth. The wound must have damaged his exquisite features, though of course his carefully curated portraits show no evidence of it. Nevertheless, he continued his progress, and soon he was advancing toward Athens, capturing two strong positions in western Attica.

On his first invasion of Athens, ten years earlier, Demetrius had stood grandly on the deck of his flagship and addressed those on shore in Piraeus, proclaiming freedom and promising gifts of grain. But those ten years had seen him ground down by losses, estranged from former friends, and driven to desperate measures. Athens too had changed, banishing him from its gates, then falling under the sway of a dictator. His strategy now aimed not at hearts or minds but at stomachs. He ravaged the fields of Attica, destroying the crops, and positioned what ships he still had to interdict shipments of food. When his crews captured a grain-supply vessel, he had its captain and steward hanged as a lesson to other importers, who quickly turned back from Piraeus. He meant to starve the city and force its tyrant Lachares to fight him, or abdicate.

Athens had endured many such food embargoes and famines, often with steely resolve. At the end of the Peloponnesian War more than a century earlier, the city had surrendered to Sparta only when its people were starving to death in the streets. So too in the current crisis, Athens put on a brave face, passing a law that mandated execution for anyone proposing negotiations with Demetrius. But conditions grew steadily worse. The prices of grain and salt rose astronomically, and the philosopher Epicurus, the head of the school that bore his name ever after, took to counting out beans to keep his students alive. In one household, as reported by Plutarch, a father and son came to blows over a mouse that fell dead from the rafters and dropped on the table between them. Still, the city held firm.

Athens could hope that like Rhodes it might receive help from

Demetrius's foes. Ptolemy sent a flotilla in aid, enough ships to get around the Antigonid blockade, but just before they arrived, Demetrius got his replacement vessels from Cyprus. With three hundred ships now in his service, he sealed off the Attic coast, completing his stranglehold. The tyrant Lachares saw that the city would have to give in and made his escape with a crew of hired soldiers. He took with him the gold and ivory cladding that Phidias, the great sculptor of Pericles' day, had attached to the cult statue of Athena in the Parthenon, a fabulous store of wealth. Phidias had crafted the statue's outer layer to be removable in case Athens needed emergency funds, yet in the century and a half since, none had dared tap it. (The theft only ensured Lachares' doom; in exile, according to Pausanias, he was killed by Boeotians who coveted his gold.)

At last there was no option left for desperate Athens. The Assembly rescinded its death-before-Demetrius law as the pro-Antigonid faction, this time led by one Dromocleides, once again took control. Envoys were sent to invite the Besieger into the city through its open gates. Demetrius, who had entered Athens first as its Savior and then as the Descender, now rode in a third time as its conqueror, accompanied by a squad of armed men. He asked that the citizens assemble in the Theater of Dionysus, the place where they usually went to see tragedies; it was just then early spring, the time of the Dionysia. Demetrius made good use of the place and the date, appearing grandly onstage as though acting the part of a mythic, tragic monarch.

The populace quaked to hear what the king might say from that stage, but Demetrius was magnanimous in victory. He rebuked the Athenians gently for rejecting him but said he was now reconciled and bore no ill will. He pledged a huge shipment of much-needed grain and a restoration of full democracy, which had been severely abridged by Lachares. The people would rule once again—

within limits of course, for Demetrius did not intend to be banished a second time. He installed a garrison force on the Hill of the Muses, at the city's southern boundary, the first such force installed in Athens itself (as opposed to the one in the lower city, Piraeus). Future Assembly meetings would be held in full view of the soldiers occupying this fortified hilltop.

The mood of the Assembly had always swung wildly when Demetrius was at issue, and now, led by Dromocleides, it swung back harder than ever toward adoration. A motion was passed that awarded Demetrius a kind of sovereignty over Piraeus, the naval base he most needed but also, as Athens well knew, the surest choke point for restricting its food supply. New strength was added to the personality cult by which Demetrius was honored as a god. Official pronouncements declared him the son of Poseidon and Aphrodite, thereby explaining both his sex appeal and his sea power. His consorts too were virtually deified; temples went up to Aphrodite Lamia and Aphrodite Leaina—two of his lovers who now become incarnations of the goddess of love. Another shrine was dedicated to Aphrodite Phila, perhaps a sign that Demetrius's daughter by Lamia had taken after her mother (unless the honoree was his wife).

What did Demetrius think of all this? Deification was much in his interest; he promoted the program himself by showing his own head on coins with the horns of a god. Yet one source reports that the Besieger expressed contempt for the self-abasement of Athens. "He marveled at these goings on and declared that not a single one of the Athenians was great or fine in spirit," reports Athenaeus, a legend collector of the second or third century CE. His account reinforces this view by quoting a scathing remark of one Duris of Samos, one of Demetrius's contemporaries. Duris noted with dismay that Athens, in its prouder days, had put its envoys to death for bowing to the ground before the Great King of Persia, yet now the city was falling all over itself to worship a much lesser king.

With Dromocleides leading the Assembly and a garrison backing him up, Demetrius departed Athens for yet more campaigning in the Peloponnese. He advanced toward Sparta this time — still a potent symbol of Hellenic vigor and might, though its power and population had been waning for decades. In a clash with the Spartan army near Mantineia, Demetrius scored a decisive win by setting a forest on fire: the smoke blew into the Spartans' eyes and obscured their vision. He took hundreds of prisoners and might have gone on to take Sparta itself, a city uncaptured, as yet, in all its long history. But he broke off the attack and went north, prompted by new developments in the land of his birth.

Events in Macedon had gone just the way the Besieger had hoped, producing a power vacuum. The tectonic plates of the post-Alexander world were shifting again, bringing opportunities for those who were nimble and willing to take Fortune's dares. But Demetrius was not the only one sensing these new avenues. Pyrrhus was also alert to the changes north of Thermopylae, and determined to benefit from them.

We last met Pyrrhus, the exiled prince of Epirus, when he went to the court of Ptolemy in Egypt as a guarantee of Demetrius's good intentions. But the death from illness of his sister Deidameia severed his kinship bond with Demetrius and weakened his allegiance to the Antigonid cause. In Alexandria he switched sides, allying with Ptolemy and abandoning Demetrius. He gained such favor at the Egyptian court that he was given Antigone, Ptolemy's stepdaughter, as his wife. Then he was given an army and money with which to reclaim his throne in Epirus, usurped years before by his cousin Neoptolemus.

Instead of fighting it out with his cousin, who had powerful allies himself, Pyrrhus accepted a truce and a power-sharing arrangement. But each man watched for a chance to do away with the other. After Pyrrhus learned that his cousin was planning to poison him, he acted first, arranging for Neoptolemus to be killed at a dinner party. The Epirotes welcomed Pyrrhus as their sole king; they had come to admire his intelligence, boldness, and dashing good looks, reminiscent for many of Alexander the Great.

Meanwhile, in neighboring Macedon, another joint-rule drama was playing out, even more sordid and deadly than events in the Epirote palace. Cassander's two surviving sons, both in their late teens or early twenties (as was Pyrrhus), were trying to share the throne, and failing badly. Their mother, Thessalonice (for whom the city in northern Greece was named), favored one of the two (Alexander), so the other (Antipater—a curse on these repurposed names!) killed her, even as she was baring her maternal breast in entreaty. Then Antipater drove his brother from power, and Alexander, from exile, sought the help of *both* Pyrrhus *and* Demetrius.

Pyrrhus was the first to respond. His army restored Alexander to power and expelled Antipater, but he exacted a steep price, carving off pieces of Macedon that neighbored his realm and installing garrisons there. The exiled Antipater landed at the court of Lysimachus, who also saw ways to enlarge his power by meddling in Macedon. He brought Antipater back to the throne just as Pyrrhus had done with Alexander, and the brothers once again agreed to share rule, each backed by his own rival dynast.

Things might have stabilized there, but Demetrius too had earlier been summoned by Alexander, and he felt entitled to take a hand in the crisis. Alexander no longer wanted him as an ally, thinking perhaps that the new power-sharing arrangement was the best he was likely to get. He also felt dread, according to Plutarch, at the approach of a man with such a huge reputation—an interesting glimpse of how Demetrius was perceived. Alexander met the Besieger at Dium, in the south of his kingdom, hoping to stop him from advancing farther. There, as narrated by Plutarch, a delicate dance of mistrust and evasion took place.

Alexander greeted Demetrius courteously but informed him that his services were no longer needed. The two kings dined together that night, but Demetrius had got wind of a plot on his life—so he *said,* anyway—and brought armed guards to the table. He also declined to drink wine, an acknowledgment of the hostile footing the two men were on. The next day, to Alexander's relief, Demetrius claimed (falsely) that he was urgently needed elsewhere and prepared to march south. Alexander escorted him into Thessaly, outside Macedonian borders. There another dinner was held, with each man warily watching the other and wondering who would strike first.

Plutarch paints a pathetic picture of young, inexperienced Alexander putting on a brave face with a man he feared while also seeking that man's elimination. At this second dinner, Alexander declined to deploy bodyguards, not wanting to demonstrate his mistrust and precipitate a showdown. But when Demetrius suddenly left the table and made for the door of his tent, Alexander knew that something was wrong. He stood up as well and ran after Demetrius, but he never caught up. As Demetrius left the tent, he told his own guards, "Strike down any one who follows me." They ran Alexander through as he reached the door, along with those who tried to come to his aid.

The tale, as Plutarch tells it, shows Demetrius acting in self-defense, for it even includes the remark of a dying courtier that "Demetrius got the jump on us by a single day." But Plutarch knew other versions of the event that said nothing of self-defense and instead described a simple first-strike assassination. The truth can never be known, for Demetrius would certainly claim that his victim intended his death even if this was a lie. Indeed he made exactly that claim before Alexander's troops after summoning them to a parley. The speech he delivered then—a version of which is preserved in one of our sources—sought to justify regicide, but also to ask for acclamation as Macedonia's king, even though Antipater still lived.

"I did not commit treachery, but rather forestalled it," Demetrius said. "Moreover, it is fitter that I be the king of the Macedonians, both by the experience that comes with age, and for other reasons." He went on to recount the histories of two fathers: his own, Antigonus One-Eye, who loyally served Alexander the Great and supported the rights of his son, and Antipater's father, Cassander, who murdered that same son and his mother, Rhoxane—indeed, the whole line of Alexander the Great—then left his own sons to pay for his crimes. Demetrius depicted himself as the agent of that vengeance, the defender, that is, of the two titanic ghosts, Philip and Alexander the Great, that now watched over their deliberations.

Defense of those ghosts and devotion to the vanished Argead line were the strongest case any speaker could make to Macedonian soldiers. The army acclaimed Demetrius as their new ruler and brought him in triumph to Pella, their capital city. Antipater, widely despised for his earlier killing of his mother, made haste to flee once again to the court of Lysimachus, where he was put to death some years later.

Demetrius took his place on the throne on which Alexander the Great had sat, the seat from which his own homeland was gov-

CHAPTER FOURTEEN

"Then Don't Be a King"

In his mid-forties, Demetrius had finally attained a stable power base and a legacy title, things he had lacked all his life. His prospects had taken a remarkable upturn since the stalemate of Rhodes and the disaster of Ipsus. The peripeties that marked his career, according to Plutarch, moved him to quote a line from a (now lost) play of Aeschylus, addressed to a personified Fortune: "You seem to both kindle my flame and blow it out." He deployed this quote, Plutarch says, at moments of failure, but he might well have noted it also applied to success.

Demetrius's coup d'état in Macedon had come not a moment too soon, for his position in the eastern Aegean had collapsed since his return to Greece. Ptolemy had moved on Cyprus and had swiftly overtaken much of the island, then put the city of Salamis under siege. Demetrius's family—Phila and his aged mother, Stratonice—had been trapped inside that city, along with much wealth and royal effects. Sidon and Tyre had already fallen by then, and Cilicia too was long gone. Demetrius could not relieve Salamis while fully committed in Greece, and the city soon fell, but Ptolemy once again showed respect for his adversary: He released Phila and his other captives and sent them to join the rest of the Antigonid clan in Europe. Demetrius, after all, was his future son-in-law, betrothed to his daughter Ptolemaïs.

Phila had been Demetrius's wife for nearly thirty years by the time of her arrival in Macedon, a loyal supporter despite her husband's philandering. Two other wives and countless mistresses (not to mention young men) had shared the Besieger's bed in those three decades. Demetrius seems to have managed to keep his subsequent partners separate from Phila, sparing her confrontations with them, though he had fathered children with at least three, Eurydice, Lamia, and Deidameia. These consorts had died or been cast off by this time, but the children lived on, a reminder to Phila of past indignities. (It didn't help matters that one of these offspring, the daughter of Lamia, bore Phila's own name.)

Like all royal wives of polygamous kings, Phila understood that her best hope lay in selflessly backing her husband's cause and raising his heir. Much to her credit, her son, young Antigonus Gonatas, now in his early twenties, had turned out a steady and spirited youth, worthy to bear the name of his revered grandfather. His mother had brought him up while his father was off campaigning, but he had learned the arts of war, and at the time of the coup he was serving as an officer in Demetrius's army. Indeed, his presence there was a part of the coup's success, for the Macedonian troops who acclaimed Demetrius noted that the king they were installing, unlike the one they were ousting, had a mature successor who was ready to take the throne.

Phila had raised a daughter as well, Stratonice, and seems to have schooled her in the patience required of would-be queen mothers. The girl had gone to Antiocheia, in Syria, after wedding Seleucus, and there had endured one of the greatest slights a wife can receive. She had borne a daughter to Seleucus, thus proving her fertility, but around the time of the Macedon coup, before she had conceived again, her husband cast her off—and married her to his *son*, Antiochus. This unprecedented, incestuous swap fascinated Greek observers, and a romantic story took hold, according to which Antiochus had fallen so deeply in love with his stepmother that a doctor thought him likely to die; Seleucus was then prevailed on against his will to give up Stratonice and let his son have her. Doubtless that tale was invented by Seleucus or one of his spinmeisters to put an attractive face on an unseemly episode. The real machinations behind the move are hard to discern.

Demetrius owed a great deal to Phila, and now that the two were at last united, and in their home country, he might have forgone further marriages. But when a message came to him from a potential new bride, Lanassa of Syracuse, Demetrius could not resist. Lanassa had left her previous husband, Pyrrhus of Epirus, on the grounds that she had too much competition from Pyrrhus's three other wives; she was then residing on Corcyra (modern Corfu), an island over which she had sovereignty. It must have pleased Demetrius greatly to be sought by Pyrrhus's ex, for his former brother-in-law was by now clearly a rival if not an outright foe. Beyond the ego gratification this marriage gave, his new bride brought with her an impressive dowry: not only Corcyra but also Leucas, a second island off Pyrrhus's western coast, was in her possession. The wedding ceremony was put on hold, however, since Demetrius had other business in hand.

With Pyrrhus as his neighbor to the west and Lysimachus to the east, Demetrius was often on campaign in the years after winning his throne. He also had to contend with rebellious Greeks. The Boeotians in particular, centered around the city of Thebes—once leveled to the ground by Alexander the Great, then restored by Cassander two decades later—were causing him numerous headaches. For unclear reasons, the Boeotians were loyal to Cassander's line and regarded Demetrius as a usurper. They mounted a rebellion against the Antigonid house, and when this was put down and punished only mildly, they revolted a second time. Possibly Lysimachus was working behind the scenes to stir them up, or else Pyrrhus was, or both.

This second Theban revolt required hard fighting. Demetrius's son Antigonus, leading troops for the first time on record, took charge of the operation for a short time while his father was busy in Thrace. (Lysimachus had briefly become a prisoner of war there after losing a battle to the Thracians; this unexpected power vacuum prompted Demetrius to invade. But the prospect of fighting Demetrius spurred the Thracians to set Lysimachus free.) Then the Besieger arrived to lead the assault in person and bring his machines to bear, for Thebes was protected by stout walls and artillery weapons. He had built another helepolis on the Boeotian plains, and now he rolled it toward Thebes, but the device was so huge that its pace was agonizingly slow. Plutarch reports a rate of progress amounting to six feet per day—credible only if one assumes that the ground beneath it was mud. Perhaps the Thebans used a trick described by Vitruvius, the Roman writer on architecture and engineering: throwing slops and sewage in front of the great machine to make its track boggy and soft. (Vitruvius says this was done at Rhodes, not Thebes, but some scholars suggest that he confused the two sieges.)

Demetrius did not wait for the great machine to arrive, but without the cover it offered led his army against the walls of Thebes. His frustration showed in the orders he gave to his men, sending them on the attack even in high-risk, low-reward situations. Antigonus, accompanying him in the field, observed with dismay the toll on the army from Theban artillery fire. He is said to have challenged his father's tactics, pointing out that too many were dying. Angrily, the Besieger shot back: "Why take it so hard? Or are you providing rations for the dead?" Apparently the young man was then in charge of the commissary. His father's cutting remark, if accurately reported by Plutarch, belittled him for worrying over losses that through attrition only made his task lighter.

The exchange shows the Besieger's nerves fraying, as he struggled over the very form of war on which his reputation was built. His son had frayed them far more by pointing out his intemperance. But Demetrius was also chastened by his son's words, according to Plutarch; he threw *himself* into the attack and incurred a serious wound, a catapult bolt to the neck. This was intemperate too, but at least the risk was his own. Despite the pain, he pressed on with the siege and finally prevailed.

Again Demetrius punished Thebes mildly, executing a dozen or so leading rebels but sparing the rest and installing a garrison. He needed the stalwart Boeotians alive, and on his side, in the greater contest to come. With every city he captured, with every political struggle resolved in his favor, Demetrius was counting up troops he could levy for a future invasion of Asia, his ultimate goal. Greece did not matter to him in itself, nor even Macedon, the place he had been born but had scarcely seen before becoming its king. These places were only springboards for the leap across the Aegean, manpower reserves to be harvested for the great anabasis. With the recapture of Thebes and the cowing of Lysimachus, the time to launch that adventure had drawn closer.

Pyrrhus, however, was still a thorn in his side. The ruler of Epirus had grown more belligerent, perhaps because Demetrius's marriage to his former wife, Lanassa—which now took place—had put him in an uncomfortable spot. Lanassa's islands Corcyra and

Leucas, as well as her powerful father, the tyrant of Syracuse, posed a threat to Pyrrhus's western coast. Demetrius seems to have thought vaguely at this juncture of forging a link to the west and even laid plans to cut a canal through the Isthmus of Corinth—creating, among other things, a path by which his fleet could attack Epirus. Such a canal would greatly speed up the transit of ships through the isthmus, accomplished up to the this point by the *diolkos,* a paved path on which they were hauled from one gulf to the other. (The Corinth canal plan, though often contemplated in ancient times, was not executed until the 1880s.)

Pyrrhus was not one to sit still while being surrounded. With Demetrius off in Corcyra celebrating his wedding, Pyrrhus orchestrated a move by his staunchest Greek allies, the Acarnanians on his southern border. These hardy hill people moved east and took parts of Phocis, including (most likely) the critical site of Apollo's oracle, Delphi; from there they threatened Thebes and even attacked Eleusis on Athenian soil, the home of the Mystery cult. Leveraging their control of Phocian mountain passes, they declared a ban on Athenian travel to Delphi, which meant the exclusion of Athens from the upcoming Pythian Games. This quadrennial athletic festival was almost as important as the one at Olympia. A city barred from the games was effectively exiled from the Hellenic family of nations.

Demetrius returned to Athens to take charge of the crisis, bringing with him his new Syracusan bride. A hymn composed for their entry into the city has been preserved entire; it reveals how far ruler-cult had advanced, and how low Athens had sunk, in the age of Demetrius. "How the greatest and dearest of gods have appeared in our city!" the hymn's author began. The other gods, says this sycophant poet, are aloof, or else have no ears to hear their petitioners; "but *you* we can see, not carved from wood or stone, but in your true form." Demetrius is the Sun, surrounded by stars, and the offspring of Poseidon and Aphrodite; the poet calls upon him to bring peace and drive out "the Aetolian Sphinx," a monster besetting Thebes, just as its mythic avatar had done. Lanassa, instantly divinized by way of her marriage, is identified with the goddess Demeter.

The hymn was performed as part of a riotous procession, according to the account of the exiled political leader Demochares (admittedly a biased source, since he had long opposed the Demetrius cult). Garlanded crowds danced and sang, poured libations of wine, and burned incense as the living deities made their way through the city's gates. Of course, such adoration implied obligation: any competent god would dispel the Aetolian threat and repair the injury to Athenian pride. Demetrius proved he was up to the challenge. Unable to open the passes in time, he simply declared that the Pythian Games would be held at *Athens* that year, not Delphi. Presumably the Greek cities he controlled—by far the majority—attended this relocated festival.

Then Demetrius went on the attack. After stopping in Macedon to gather more troops, he invaded Aetolia, forcing the inhabitants to flee to their mountain redoubts. (It was in Aetolia, we recall, that more than thirty years earlier Demetrius had begun his storied career, accompanying his father on the embassy to Antipater and Craterus.) Leaving an army there to pursue the campaign, he went on the hunt for Pyrrhus, who was also hunting for him. The two commanders somehow marched past one another, so a showdown never took place, but Pyrrhus embarrassed Demetrius by defeating the force left in Aetolia and taking thousands of prisoners. The loss of troops was irksome but the loss of face was a bigger concern. Unlike Demetrius's other rivals—by now approaching their eighties—Pyrrhus was a man of his own stamp, bold, handsome, aggressive, and young. Some said it was Pyrrhus, not he, who could give the world what it longed for, a new Alexander.

Campaigning against rivals like Pyrrhus suited Demetrius far better than governing on the domestic front. Back in his native land, his subjects were growing unhappy with the king their army had chosen. In the few spans of time when Demetrius dwelt among them, he showed his disdain for their pleas and petitions; once he collected an armload of these, then was spotted a short while later dumping them from a bridge into the river Axios. He kept ambassadors waiting interminably and after admitting them often became harsh and impatient. His every gesture and utterance revealed his contempt for his duties.

One old Macedonian woman had the nerve to call Demetrius out for his high-handed ways. She approached him as he passed by in the street and demanded a hearing, only to be told, "I haven't the time." "*Then don't be a king,*" she replied. Plutarch reports that Demetrius, stung by this comment, immediately gave several days to hearing petitions, including that of the old woman. But the turnabout clearly had not come from a real change of heart.

For all that he disappointed them, the Macedonians, especially the soldiers, were loyal to Demetrius and to his son Antigonus, now clearly a capable heir. They stuck by him when he suddenly fell ill, in 289, and Pyrrhus seized the moment to invade the Macedonian heartland. A small push by the army at that moment would have easily toppled Demetrius, but the men stood by his side. The Besieger rose from his sickbed to meet the invasion and drive Pyrrhus out, inflicting heavy losses. Thereafter the two kings signed a truce that preserved the peace and the status quo.

Such skirmishes must have vexed the Besieger as much as the petty requests of his subjects. The jousts with Pyrrhus and Lysimachus were an annoying distraction from his real goal, the only goal that mattered, the great anabasis—a march into Asia by "going up" from the coast. He was getting nearer that goal, amassing soldiers and horses, stockpiling rations, and most of all building ships by the hundreds in Athens, Corinth, and his own capital, Pella. He oversaw the work at the dockyards in person, supervising new vessels of larger and larger design, including fifteeners, the largest aquatic craft yet built, and the long-range artillery weapons affixed to their decks. Soon he had five hundred ships either complete or in progress, enough to transport an army of over a hundred thousand.

Such a force could win back the empire that had once been his father's, perhaps even the one that had been Alexander's. But such a force could not be amassed in secret.

Word filtered back to the other Successors of what was afoot: an armada that might destroy each of them, one by one. The first to be taken down, clearly, would be Lysimachus, then either Ptolemy or Seleucus, depending on whether Demetrius turned east or south. The last of the three would have to face an army augmented by the troops of both of the others.

It must have seemed absurd to these men that they still had to fear Demetrius after the crushing defeat they dealt him at Ipsus. But the man's will to power had proved adamantine, defying all expectations. Once more they banded together and formed an anti-Antigonid league, recruiting Pyrrhus in place of the dead Cassander. Pyrrhus had just signed a nonaggression pact with Demetrius but they persuaded him to break it, in part by twitting him over his loss of Lanassa, but mostly by warning him that his own reign was at stake as much as theirs were. If one domino fell, the others were sure to follow.

CHAPTER FIFTEEN

The Unraveling

As he approached his fiftieth year, at the height of his power, Demetrius looked every inch a king, adorned with gold and purple from head to toe. On his feet he wore specially made purple slippers embroidered with gold; his headdress was a purple-dyed version of the traditional Macedonian *kausia*, a broad-brimmed hat, encircled by a gold diadem that served as the crown of that day. His robe, too, was purple and gold, but he was having a new one made, even more grand, embroidered with the sun, the stars, and the signs of the zodiac. He meant to cast himself as lord of the cosmos. According to Plutarch, the grandiosity of this garment proved an embarrassment to Demetrius's descendants, none of whom ventured to wear it.

Such adornments were usually seen, in the Greek world at least, only on the tragic stage, where actors impersonated the kings of mythic times. There was indeed something theatrical about Demetrius, as Plutarch notes in his description of the king's garb. He often seemed to be fitting himself to a tragic role, especially that of Alexander the Great, the hero whose life had conformed to a dramatist's art. Athenian flatterers had lifted Demetrius even higher, asking him to play the part of a god. But with his military stumbles and character flaws, he kept proving that he was human — all too human — and no Alexander. The last phase of his life was to bring the greatest proofs of this.

Theatrical displays might awe the general public, but to tough, professional soldiers, only one thing marked out the hero of mythic stature: success on the field of battle. In the early-third-century world, huge numbers of men made a living fighting for one or another of the Successors, and they looked to their livelihoods with a practiced eye. The general who led them to wins and enriched them with plunder was the man they were glad to call king. Demetrius was increasingly falling short of this measure; at the siege of Thebes his own son had thought he was wasting the lives of his troops. He had grown aloof and imperious with age. His troops had started to sense *barutes*, harshness or severity, coming from him, in a way they deeply disliked.

The flaws of Demetrius stood out in higher relief when compared with the virtues of his neighbor Pyrrhus, his major rival in the contest for Greek allegiance. Among the Epirotes, his own people, Pyrrhus was hailed as "the Eagle," and he graciously told them they had made him an eagle by lifting him up on the "wings" of their weapons. When he marched into Macedon during Demetrius's illness, he drew defections even from those whose homeland he was invading. The word was getting around in armed camps that Pyrrhus was *philostratiotes*, a friend to the fighting man. Pyrrhus himself was spreading that word by way of Epirote infiltrators dressed as Macedonians.

Pyrrhus had a key role to play in the plan to destroy Demetrius. He was to invade Macedon again, from the west, while Lysimachus charged in from the east; Ptolemy, meanwhile, would send ships up from the south to foment rebellion in the cities of Greece and the islands. Seleucus was too far away to attack but would lend his support, in part by refraining from seizing lands from the others. Demetrius would have war on three fronts, and nowhere to run if he took to his ships, many of which were not yet ready for launching.

When it began, the attack seems to have caught Demetrius by surprise. His eyes were so fixed on his own grand plan, the invasion of Asia, that he failed to anticipate this preemptive strike. Nor had he foreseen that Pyrrhus, his western neighbor, might pose a threat, since the two had only recently signed their nonaggression pact. Such pacts were often violated with ease, but this one must have had more teeth, for Pyrrhus had consented to break it only after Ptolemy and the others had fairly besieged him with letters and ambassadorial missions. So says Plutarch, but his account too might have arisen as propaganda, designed to put a good face on what was clearly betrayal.

It was spring or early summer 288 when Demetrius learned of the double-cross and the double invasion of Macedon from east and from west. He abandoned his tours of the dockyards and hastened to meet the threat, leaving Antigonus in southern Greece to keep the cities in line. He moved first against Lysimachus and defeated him at Amphipolis, but the win was not decisive. Meanwhile, far to the west, Pyrrhus advanced into Macedon and captured Berroia, an important strategic point, without a fight. Demetrius was caught between hammer and anvil, just as his foes had planned.

When the fall of Berroia was learned in Demetrius's camp, all hell broke loose. The image Demetrius had tried to project of mythic and godlike power had been revealed as a hoax. His Macedonian troops gave vent to their grief and scorn, hurling curses at their king and vowing to leave his service; some did indeed leave, pretending to return to their homes but in fact deserting to Lysimachus. Demetrius saw that he must get clear of this foe before losing more of his forces. He decided to lead them against Pyrrhus instead, hoping perhaps to fare better there in the tug-of-war of defections; despite his charisma, Pyrrhus was still a Greek and thus, in the eyes of the Macedonian troops, a foreigner. So Demetrius marched his remaining troops westward and camped near Berroia, seeking to restore his plummeting reputation.

Pyrrhus understood what was at stake. He spread a report of a dream he had had, in which he was summoned by Alexander the Great. In the dream, Alexander was lying on a couch as though ailing; he'd spoken to Pyrrhus in kindly tones, vowing to help him achieve victory. "And how can you help, being ill?" Pyrrhus asked. "With my very name," Alexander replied, then leapt from the couch and rode off on a cavalry horse as though charging into a battle. A dream like this had served Seleucus well when he took Babylon away from Antigonus One-Eye; now Pyrrhus hoped to take Macedon away from Demetrius.

The deceptions and rumored dream had their intended effect. Demetrius's soldiers felt they beheld in Pyrrhus the qualities their own king lacked, and many snuck off to his camp. They deserted in small groups at first and in secret, but finally left en masse and without concealment, searching for Pyrrhus so they could surrender themselves, binding oak boughs to their helmets as they saw the Epirotes do. None knew as yet what Pyrrhus looked like and they could not find him until he put on his distinctive helmet with its high horsehair crest and goat's horns. Then they flocked to him and pledged themselves to his cause.

Amid the desolation of a collapsing camp, a few trusted friends came to Demetrius and advised him, in the gentlest terms they could find, that abdication might not be unwise. It did not take much to persuade him. His armed strength had melted away from beneath him, without a blow being struck. It was too late now to regret the petitions not heard, the citizens ignored or insulted, the soldiers' lives thrown away in the siege of Thebes. Demetrius cast off his battle gear and his royal attire, donned a simple soldier's cloak and Macedonian hat, and stole away from the scene. In an instant, as unexpectedly as it began, his six-year reign as Macedon's monarch was over.

With Demetrius gone, the few remaining soldiers in camp tore apart his royal tent and plundered its gear, fighting for precious objects worth a lifetime of campaigning. Then Pyrrhus arrived to take control of the camp and the tent. Many in Macedon now wanted him as their king, but Pyrrhus was wary of their changes of mood, and also wary of Lysimachus. The lord of Thrace had shared the burdens of war and felt that he deserved a share of the spoils. So they split Macedon down the middle and each absorbed half into his own kingdom. This meant that, as Plutarch observes in a meditation on the endless desire for power, they would inevitably soon be at war with one another.

Demetrius had lost Macedon but not southern Greece. He still had control of key cities, including Athens, and still had ships, harbors, and money to hire rowers. He made his way incognito to Cassandreia, a town in the Chalcidice, to join his wife Phila, who was in residence there. He had been cast down before, after Ipsus, yet managed to bounce back; he could do so again, he felt sure, and complete the plan, so cruelly cut short by his foes, for the great anabasis. No doubt he repeated, as he made his way toward his wife, the line from Aeschylus he had made his personal motto, the one about Fortune snuffing out his flame but then, when all seemed darkest, blowing it back into a blaze.

Phila, however, did not have the same faith in Fortune's restor-

CHAPTER SIXTEEN

A King in Plain Clothes

Athens had watched events in the North with intense concern, aware once again of how much the city's fate was linked to that of Demetrius. A squad of Antigonid troops still resided on the Hill of the Muses to keep the Athenian government in line. The pro-Demetrian party had controlled that government for seven years, ensuring honors for the Besieger that made him one of the gods. But what sort of god had his throne yanked away from beneath him without even striking a blow?

In Piraeus, a huge fleet of Demetrius's ships rode at anchor or were hauled up into ship sheds; still others were under construction. The harbor town belonged to Demetrius, by decree of the Assembly, and he had secured his hold on it with a second garrison. Two decades earlier, he had taken Piraeus by force, standing on the deck of his ship to proclaim liberation. Now it was *he* from whom the Athenians—a large number at least—sought to be liberated. In the wake of his debacle in Macedon, Athens once again changed tack, as it had after Ipsus, and prepared to rid itself of its so-called Savior.

Demetrius was back in Greece at this point, visiting cities he still controlled to shore up support. He dressed no longer in purple and gold but affected the style of a private citizen. Someone who saw him at Thebes wittily quoted two of the opening lines of Euripides' *Bacchae*. In that famous play, Dionysus returns to Thebes from abroad in disguise to spread his rites and punish those who have refused to accept him as a divinity. At the play's outset he appears onstage and proclaims that he has "exchanged the appearance of god for that of a man"—a perfect fit for the plainclothes Demetrius. It remained to be seen whether the ending of the play, in which Dionysus destroys a king who failed to worship him, would also become an apt parallel.

Athens had been starved into submission the previous time it rebelled, and the same thing might happen again if the city was unprepared. The fields of Attica were full of ripe grain in the spring of 287, the moment Athens decided to again cast off its Antigonid yoke. A huge effort was needed to gather the harvest before the Macedonian troops could take action. Reapers were turned out by military roll-call so that all the strongest hands would be put to work. But events spun out of control. The garrison troops realized what was at stake and tried to use force to prevent the collection of grain—a clear indication of what lay ahead. Demetrius meant to once again put a choke hold around the city and starve it into submission.

But Athens had friends in this fight, among them a captain in the employ of Ptolemy. The lord of Egypt had sent his fleet north as part of the joint operation against Demetrius, and that fleet had occupied some Cycladic islands, including Andros. An Athenian was in Ptolemy's service there, Callias of Sphettus, a rich man and a friend of the anti-Demetrian faction. When he learned of the nascent revolt and the race to collect the grain, Callias used his own wealth to pay a thousand mercenaries to sail for Attica and defend the harvesters. He himself incurred a wound in the fight, but his men ensured that the grain was brought in. Later the city awarded Callias a gold wreath for his service, as told in a long stone inscription that attests to much of what happened in the revolt.

As the struggle over the grain played out in the fields, a different contest took shape within the walls of Athens. Gathering those few soldiers not already deployed, the Athenians' new commander, a former pro-Demetrian now turned anti-, led an attack on the garrison atop the Hill of the Muses. The officer commanding that fort, a certain Strombichus, switched sides, abandoned his post, and brought some of his troops over with him. These men were in Demetrius's employ but had lived for years in the shade of the Parthenon and other landmarks of the greatness of Athens. When forced to choose they could no longer support the Besieger's ugly plan to keep the world's freest city under the heel of his boot.

The remaining garrison troops withdrew to the Hill of the Muses, their fortified base, and hunkered down to await the Besieger's arrival. They did not wait long. Demetrius had been in the Peloponnese when the revolt of Athens broke out, and drawing on his many allies there, he scraped together a sizable army. Soon he arrived with that army outside the gates. Those in the city who remembered the nightmares of 295, when a father and son had come to blows over a dead mouse, saw the same horror beginning again. But now there was a new player in the geopolitical game. The Athenians sent a distress call to Pyrrhus, no friend of freedom himself but a foe to Demetrius.

The Besieger camped outside the walls of Athens, prepared to conduct yet another fantastical siege operation. He had battered by now at the walls of Salamis, Sidon, Rhodes, Messene, Thebes, and plenty of smaller places; some he had taken, at others he had failed. Perhaps by this time a joke that later spread widely was already getting around: that he was called poliorcetes, Besieger, because he put cities to siege but did not, in fact, capture them. Now a new challenge was before him and a chance to batter down the ramparts of Athens, the scaling ladder of Greece, as his father's friends had termed it. That metaphor was a potent one for a man who had set scaling ladders on many a wall.

But his father had quashed that metaphor and instead called Athens a beacon, broadcasting Antigonid virtues throughout the Greek world. Did Demetrius want this beacon broadcasting his cruelty? The question became paramount as envoys came forth from the city: a group of philosophers, led by one Crates, approached him, seeking a parley. Perhaps this was Crates the Cynic, a Gandhi-like wise man who gave away his family fortune so as not to be tainted by wealth, and was called "Open-Door-Man" because everyone welcomed him into their homes. If it was this Crates who now came forward, the Athenians had chosen their representative well. Demetrius stayed his hand, perhaps shamed by Crates; the approach of Pyrrhus, no doubt, also played on his mind.

Another diplomat, one of Ptolemy's men, arrived in Piraeus soon after to negotiate a stand-down. Athens offered generous terms: Demetrius could keep his hold on Piraeus, as well as his forts in the Attic countryside, in exchange for lifting the siege and assuring Athens of freedom. The city had already removed his partisans from high office and elected their own magistrates, restoring a sense that the people were back in control. The shrines of the Savior Gods still stood, but they had fewer visitors now. Demetrius's star was on the wane, but he had kept what he needed: Piraeus, a nearly impregnable naval base with shipyards and docks. He could still rely on his fleet, including the two newly built giant warships — if only he could man them with oarsmen and fill them with troops.

At some point Pyrrhus arrived on the scene, also inclined to negotiate rather than fight. He signed a separate peace with Demetrius, though neither could have much trusted the other at this point. While in the region Pyrrhus paid an honorary visit to Athens and climbed the Acropolis to sacrifice to the city's patron goddess, Athena. The Athenians took the measure of this new regional strongman, the king of a land that to them was the wild frontier, and he of them, the superpower of the past, now wholly dependent on others. He remarked, as he prepared to depart, that though he was glad to have helped the Athenians, he thought they would do well to never again admit any king through their gates — a ban that included himself.

Somewhere amid these comings and goings, unseen in our sources, Antigonus, son of Demetrius, kept watch on the family's Greek holdings. He had become his father's trusted field agent, just as his father had once been for *his* father. All the Successors by now were deploying their sons in this way: Lysimachus had Agathocles, Seleucus Antiochus, and Ptolemy two Ptolemy Juniors, sons born to different wives. The elder of the two, Ptolemy Ceraunus, "Thunderbolt," departed Egypt at the time of Demetrius's siege of Athens, disturbed by the preferences shown to his younger half-brother. He landed at the court of Lysimachus, where we shall meet him again in due course.

These sons all stood to inherit their fathers' kingdoms, as well as their fathers' grudges and enmities. The Wars of the Successors would pass to a new generation, and Antigonus Gonatas would uphold his family's claims in a way that would have made Demetrius proud. But that tale too belongs to a later chapter.

Though he had been ejected from Macedon and stymied at Athens, Demetrius was hardly a beaten man. Many in Greece still believed in his cause, or at least believed there were gains to be grabbed in his train. Eleven thousand signed on for his Asian adventure or were impressed into service. This was a tiny force compared to what he had planned, but large enough to make inroads against his rivals and raise cash by raiding and slaving; the cash could then pay for more troops. He was not yet ready to launch a full-scale anabasis, but little by little he might claw his way back to his former strength. Then he would show the world what a new Alexander could do, with his giant ships and machines, his wealth and magnificence, his ceaseless ambition.

Leaving his son to govern the Greeks in his absence, Demetrius crossed the Aegean one final time, heading for Anatolia and the lands of Lysimachus.

CHAPTER SEVENTEEN

The Great Anabasis

As soon as Demetrius had departed for Asia, Pyrrhus broke the pact the two had just made and invaded Thessaly, Antigonid turf. Plutarch in his life of Pyrrhus notes an interesting reason for this betrayal. "Pyrrhus found the Macedonians easier to manage when they were on campaign than when they had no task in hand," Plutarch writes. "And he himself was not disposed by nature toward idleness." The comment could equally well apply to Demetrius, or, indeed, to any of the Successors.

For Pyrrhus and Demetrius, as for Alexander the Great, military life was a kind of addiction, a set of rituals and patterns from which it was hard to break free. All three men had been trained in these patterns from their teenage years: the endless cycle of striking camp, marching, and pitching camp again, punctuated by the adrenalized thrill of the battle. The rough fellowship of an all-male world, the license of a society not bound by laws were an intoxication. Few who grew accustomed to it ever left it behind. Even after completing the conquest of half of the world, Alexander, on the eve of his death, was planning a further campaign, and more beyond that, to subdue the other half as well. No end to the fight was in view.

But a leader's obsessions always cost the lives of his men. Alexander had seen this in Gedrosia, the cruel and harbor-less coast shared today by Pakistan and Iran, a place without food or freshwater. Returning from his eastern campaign, Alexander had marched his men through this trackless waste, though other, less perilous routes stood open. He lost hundreds, perhaps thousands, to hunger, thirst, and exhaustion. He blamed the disaster on failed supply lines, but many of his veterans knew better. Yet they followed him still, for they too, after twelve years or more in the field, were addicted and no longer sought a life outside the camp. When Alexander ordered a large contingent sent home, the men mutinied rather than be decommissioned.

Demetrius's generation, and even more that of Pyrrhus, was rife with such addicts, for the Wars of the Successors had drawn huge numbers away from homes and farms and into the soldiery. Standing armies, once a rare innovation, had by now become a feature of all the Successor states. And armies needed goals to pursue, as Plutarch observed; inactivity bred disaffection. The Diadoch Wars became what today we call a feedback loop: the more men who enrolled, the more the fighting expanded, creating the need for more men. The costs of defeat were light by modern standards; the winning general did not seek a high casualty rate, for the troops who survived, in most cases, would became *his* troops, in the hope of faring better the next time around.

Among those who crossed the Aegean with Demetrius on his final crusade, some were men of this stamp, adventurers and career soldiers inured to the life of the camp. Others were inductees, pressed into service from Greek cities controlled by Demetrius. A few perhaps were believers, who saw the king and his son as the best hope to control the empire's center and stabilize the world order. Certainly none of the other dynasts seemed able to link Europe together with Asia, except perhaps Lysimachus, but he was widely disliked and was now nearing eighty.

Thus it was that with hopes of plunder, of a better world to come, or of mere survival, eleven thousand embarked with Demetrius in the spring of 286 and set sail for the Anatolian coast. Very few, as things turned out, would see their homelands again.

As he had done after Ipsus, Demetrius moved to attack Lysimachus, the most accessible of his opponents and, in some ways, the weakest. The rich lands of western Anatolia belonged to Lysimachus, but he inspired little loyalty or affection there; by contrast the line of Antigonus One-Eye, a man still warmly remembered, could inspire devotion. Plutarch records that in Phrygia, One-Eye's former home territory, the memory of the old regime was still cherished. A farmer seen digging a hole there was asked by a passerby what he was doing; he replied, "I'm looking for Antigonus." Such sympathies could help Demetrius bring over the cities of Asia to his cause. He started in Caunus, a place already friendly to him, and worked his way up the coast, with the fleet keeping pace alongside.

In Miletus, Demetrius found a friendly reception and what was more, a long-awaited royal bride. Ptolemaïs, Ptolemy's daughter, who was betrothed to him ten years previously, met him there and the two at last were wed, the fifth marriage for Demetrius but the first for the young woman. The circumstances are vague, but it is probable that Ptolemy sanctioned the match, regarding Demetrius as more of an asset than a threat. The prospects now of Demetrius invading Egypt were remote, whereas the harm he was doing to Lysimachus, and might later do to Seleucus, was much in Ptolemy's interest. The bride was the niece of Phila, Demetrius's first wife, and thus Demetrius's niece as well, though not related by blood.

Ephesus too went over to the side of Demetrius, who promptly garrisoned it, but Lysimachus got it back with a clever trick. A pirate named Andro (or Mandro) was raiding in nearby waters and bringing his plunder back to Ephesus for sale. But Lycus, an officer serving Lysimachus, bribed the pirate to lead a squad of soldiers into the city disguised as prisoners destined for slave marts. The "slaves" were led up to the garrison fort, where they suddenly drew concealed weapons and slew Demetrius's men. The pirate chief got his pay but was banned from Ephesus thereafter on grounds he could not be trusted. The city went back to Lysimachan control.

Demetrius turned inland from the coast and took Sardis, a wealthy and strategically important city. His campaign was gaining momentum, and some of Lysimachus's officers came over to his side. But his very success meant that others aligned against him, the pattern that had plagued the Antigonids from the beginning. Demetrius had counted on enmity between Pyrrhus and Lysimachus to keep the latter busy in Europe, but these two had now struck a pact of collaboration. Secure for the moment at home, Lysimachus dispatched his son Agathocles with a sizable army and orders to drive Demetrius out of his lands. And that was the start of the expedition's downfall.

The arrival of Agathocles on the Anatolian coast cut Demetrius off from his ships and from any hope of resupply from Europe. Demetrius might have risked a battle, but didn't; evidently he lacked troop strength — or confidence in the loyalty of his men. Instead he withdrew into Phrygia, but Agathocles pursued him. Demetrius saw now that he would have to head east, to Seleucus's realm, and try to raise troops in sectors where some of his father's loyalists had been settled. He kept this plan secret, for his men had signed on for a coastal campaign and would not have wanted to go so far from the sea. Nonetheless, some began to suspect his intentions. The camp grew uneasy.

The central Anatolian plateau, which the army was crossing, had little to offer in the way of grain crops. Demetrius could get neither forage nor shipments from home—wherever "home" was at this point. Food stocks began to run short, the same situation that had led to disaster for Alexander the Great in Gedrosia. The Antigonid troops were forced to eat unaccustomed foods, Plutarch says, though without recording what these were. In similar straits other armies had first consumed their own pack animals and cavalry horses, then grass and local vegetation. Whatever Demetrius's men were eating made many of them ill, contributing to the growing decline in morale.

Weak from hunger and malnutrition, the troops had to cross a fast-running river, the Lycus, in central Anatolia. Surviving reports diverge on what happened there: In his *Stratagems*, Polyaenus, collector of tactical exempla, credits Demetrius with a successful crossing in which horses were used to break the force of the current. But Plutarch gives a more dire account, claiming a number of troops were swept away and drowned. Perhaps the two writers are speaking of different rivers and one of them got the name wrong. If Plutarch's account is correct, then Demetrius committed an error of judgment, sending his men into harm's way, or else he was so pressed by hunger or pursuit that he had no choice.

The troops began to wonder where their commander was heading and whether he had any sort of plan. One of them gave voice to his doubts by quoting the opening lines from a play of Sophocles. At the start of *Oedipus at Colonus*, the title figure, blind and ragged, old and feeble, comes onstage led by his daughter Antigone and asks, "Child of a blind father, Antigone, / What lands have we come to, or what cities of men?" With the change of a single syllable, the anonymous soldier made the lines fit nearly perfectly: "Child of a blind father, Antigonus . . . " Demetrius's father had been blind only in one eye, but the spoof was ingenious, offering a rare moment of levity in a desperate situation.

The man who had formerly dressed as a tragic monarch, with theatrically grand purple robes and gold crowns, had now become a tragic exile instead, cast out of his homeland and wandering lost and resourceless. Like the aged Oedipus, he was cursed by his past sins, the blows he had struck against each of the other dynasts. To whom could he turn for help? The Greeks of Thebes and the Peloponnese were his last remaining allies, but they were far off across the Aegean, a sea from which he was barred by Agathocles. He could only hope that Seleucus, his erstwhile son-in-law, might look on him with pity, if only for the sake of Stratonice, now married to Seleucus's son, and the children she had borne, in whom the two royal bloodlines were united.

Desperate to reach lands where his men could find food, Demetrius crossed the Taurus Mountains and came through the Cilician Gates, a narrow pass leading into a fertile plain. The transit took a horrific toll: Plutarch reports that *eight thousand* were lost in this stage of the journey, a staggering figure if true. No doubt the count includes desertions, for many must have run off to join Agathocles, whose army was not far behind. Once his quarry moved south of the Taurus range, Agathocles felt that his job was accomplished: he had pushed Demetrius out of Lysimachan territory and into the lands of Seleucus. He locked the Gates shut with a guard post and went home to Thrace.

Demetrius found himself back in Cilicia, a region he had occupied twice and been twice booted out of. He had attacked it when it had belonged to Pleistarchus, Cassander's brother, and Seleucus, at that time his son-in-law, had not intervened. But now it was Seleucus who owned the region. Demetrius shrank from despoiling the lands of the last man on earth who might help him, but he could not hold back troops who needed to plunder or die. As the ravaging began, Demetrius sent a long letter to Seleucus, explaining the situation and asking for clemency. He had suffered enough, he wrote, to deserve some measure of pity even from foes — and Seleucus was surely not a foe, he implied.

Or was he? The relationship of these two had become quite complex since the days they had feasted together on an Antigonid flagship. The marital bond they had struck in those days had been partly dissolved, though not completely since Stratonice was now Seleucus's daughter-in-law. Seleucus had cast her off unwillingly, to save his son's life — or so said the tale that was going around. Had Seleucus put out that story himself to avoid the appearance of a rift? Was Demetrius still too well liked in the world, and his father too fondly remembered, for Seleucus to reject him openly?

Such are the mysteries of the age of the Successors, often beyond our powers of inquiry. We would give a lot to read that letter from Demetrius to Seleucus, or to know in what frame of mind Seleucus perused it. What is clear, though, from his subsequent actions is that he walked a fine line in dealing with Demetrius, not wishing to either embrace him or destroy him. And when he did act against the man with whom he shared grandchildren, he put out reports (or someone put them out for him) that shifted the blame onto others. For the public, it seems, did not want to see Demetrius wronged, despite all the wrongs the man himself had committed.

From this effort at spin, as it seems, comes the tale of what happened next. Seleucus read the letter and (as Plutarch's account describes) was moved to deep sympathy. He instructed his officers near Cilicia to treat Demetrius like a king and supply all needed provisions to his starving troops. But then a courtier named Patrocles stepped forward. A skilled military engineer, this man had helped Seleucus defend Babylon from Demetrius, decades earlier, by using irrigation canals to flood the surrounding fields. Patrocles now convinced the court that Demetrius was dangerous, full of aggression and sure to misbehave in desperate straits. Seleucus hearkened to Patrocles' warnings and changed his tack. He went to confront Demetrius at the head of an army.

More likely what had really transpired was this: Seleucus wanted to keep Demetrius off guard and so sent him a deferential message, all the while arming to fight him. It was precisely what Antigonus One-Eye had done with the Arabs of Petra to enable Demetrius, then a young man, to take them by surprise. If this was what took place, then — again according to Plutarch — the trick worked. Demetrius was expecting succor and kindness when his scouts reported Seleucus approaching in battle array.

That report sent the Besieger into despair. He wrote again to Seleucus, or perhaps held a parley in person, and made a set of requests that showed how far he had fallen. He asked now for only a tiny realm in the Taurus Mountains, where he could reign over poor barbarian tribes and cause no more trouble to any of the Successors. That at least would give him a kingdom to be king *of.* But if even this could not be, he begged Seleucus, then might his army at least have food for the coming winter? Or must he be brought to the nadir, driven back toward Lysimachus, destitute, with no way to feed himself or his men, and winter coming on, a winter many would not survive?

Seleucus mistrusted his former father-in-law but was not entirely deaf to this plea. He offered Demetrius refuge for two months, the heart of the winter, in a place called Cataonia, a less consequential region than Cilicia. That rugged land might yield enough sustenance to preserve life but not enough to help him rebuild his fortunes. Even this meager offer came with a condition: Demetrius had to provide his chief officers as hostages, ensuring his good behavior with their lives.

Demetrius no doubt recalled the day when he had made the same demand of the Rhodians, under threat of total war. He had delivered many ultimatums in his career, only to end up on the receiving end. Plutarch spares his dignity by not recording his reply to Seleucus, though he must have acceded, then made his desolate way into Cataonia.

No one at that point could guess what direction he might move after winter was over or what he planned next. Seleucus sent troops to close off the passes that led into Syria to prevent him from making incursions there. The two men disengaged and went separate ways. They had not resolved the question of what their relations would be, or whether their intertwined family lines would prevent a fatal collision. No doubt both men sensed that answers would have to emerge soon enough.

CHAPTER EIGHTEEN

Twists of the Knife

As word spread of Demetrius's difficulties, his subjects and allies throughout the eastern Mediterranean began to defect. Many had suffered under taxes imposed for the great anabasis; some had been kept in line by means of garrisons and armed troops. Having started out as their liberator, Demetrius had become their oppressor. Sidon and Tyre and the fleets they harbored soon deserted his cause, going over to Ptolemy once again after being retaken from him. Farther north, Miletus opened its gates to Lysimachus. The last remnants of the naval empire were quickly falling away.

In mainland Greece, Antigonus Gonatas struggled to keep what little was left of his father's European assets. His principal base was Piraeus, controlled by the garrison fort of Munychia, where a captain named Heraclides commanded two thousand men. Antigonus counted on them to keep the harbor in his family's hands, for Athens, he knew, was eager to get it back. Indeed, with the help of funds supplied by Ptolemy and Lysimachus, Athenians had already won back from him other positions, including the valuable fortress at Eleusis.

In the previous year, Athens had overthrown a different garrison force, that on the Hill of the Muses, by suborning an officer and persuading him to defect. The same trick was now attempted in Piraeus on a man named Hierocles. Athenian agents contacted him in the Attic countryside, where he was attending a festival, and bribed him to open the gates of the Munychia fort at night and let in a squad of Athenian troops. These would assassinate Heraclides before the alarm could be raised. But Hierocles took a lesson from the captain at Rhodes who had won gold and glory by way of a double-cross. He disclosed the plot to Heraclides, who prepared his forces to strike. On the night in question, 420 Athenians stole into the fort and were slaughtered to a man.

By these measures Antigonus kept control of Piraeus, along with Thebes, Corinth, and parts of the Peloponnese. He had done what he had been asked to do: maintain the family's positions in Greece while Demetrius took ship for Asia. But with two foes pressing him from the north, Lysimachus and Pyrrhus, he could not spare any troops to aid his beleaguered father, and in any case all the crossings to Asia were in enemy hands. Cut off from his son by land and by sea, Demetrius would have to fight on alone — whatever it was he was fighting for at this point.

The winter in Cataonia must have been brutal, though Plutarch supplies no details. He says only that Demetrius had become "like a wild beast, hemmed in and pelted from all sides." Demetrius was not yet actually being pelted, but like a trapped lion or boar assailed by hunters' spears, he was desperate to find a way out and willing to take any chance.

At the start of spring Demetrius again led his band into Cilicia on plundering raids, perhaps to ensure their continuing loyalty. This time he apparently did not write to Seleucus; there was little point any longer. In skirmishes with Seleucus's garrison troops, Demetrius had the best of things, even though scythe-bearing chariots—a fearsome anti-personnel device adopted from the East—were launched against him by the Seleucid troops.

Using guerrilla tactics, Demetrius made small inroads and even gained control of the Amanic Gates, an important pass leading east from Cilicia. By way of this pass he could plunder another Seleucid land, Cyrrhestica, a fertile and populous region. Macedonian settlers there, he hoped, might flock to his cause, stirred by the high name of his father, who had once led them. But just when his fortunes seemed to be on the rise, Demetrius fell ill again, as he had in Macedonia some years previously.

Probably Demetrius, like many in his day, had chronic malaria, a disease that stays dormant for long stretches but causes fevers and desperate fatigue whenever it reemerges. For forty days he lay prostrate while his soldiers, dismayed at his downturn, began to desert in large numbers. He was left with perhaps a few thousand, hardened troops for the most part who did not object to the outlaw life, together with a few steadfast friends, the last true believers in the Antigonid cause.

With such a small force Demetrius at least had speed and stealth on his side. When he recovered his strength he feigned a return to Cilicia, then doubled back in the night and went through the Amanic Gates. He seems to have aimed for the city of Cyrrhus, a place founded by his father, to raise more troops from the veterans there, or simply to give his desperadoes fresh plunder. In either case he could guess that Seleucus would soon be upon him, but he had a plan to deal with his foe — one that relied, as did so many plans in this era, on secrecy and surprise: a night attack that would terrify Seleucus's army into surrender.

Seleucus himself had shown how effective this plan could be. In his own campaign to retake Babylon, leading only a few thousand men, he had surprised the much larger army sent against him by launching a night attack. His foes had laid down their arms, then joined Seleucus's ranks, instantly quintupling his troop strength. Such a coup was the best hope Demetrius had, and his men agreed that the trick was worth trying. When they learned that Seleucus had camped nearby, they set off in the dark, taking care not to make undue noise or light any torches. They had come fairly close to their goal when they suddenly heard the blare of trumpets and saw fires blazing all over Seleucus's camp.

Demetrius had been betrayed. Two Aetolians in his army had run on ahead and, reaching Seleucus's guardsmen, insisted on being taken to see their commander. Seleucus had been jolted awake when he heard their report, and instantly ordered the trumpets blown and the fires lit. The ruckus made it clear his army was ready to fight, even in darkness. Demetrius had too few to engage without the advantage of surprise; he had to abandon his plan. He called off the attack and withdrew. The man who had failed by hours in Egypt, and by inches at Rhodes, had once again fallen just short.

Seleucus led his army in pursuit, and Demetrius elected to stand and fight. It seems he had found a narrows in which his small force would be bounded by high ground on either side and could not be outflanked. What followed is only a blur in the two brief descriptions we have, those of Plutarch and Polyaenus, but the outcome is clear enough.

Demetrius fought on the right wing of his line, and apparently had some success there against Seleucus's troops. But Seleucus took a squad of picked men and eight elephants, and made his way around to Demetrius's left. When he came within sight of the hungry, exhausted men stationed there, he took off his helmet, revealing his face. He wanted the men to know who he was, and also to see his elephants, a weapon they were in no condition to fight. Then he addressed them, in words preserved (or imagined) by Polyaenus.

"How long will you be so mad as to stick by a bandit," he asked, "who has nothing for you to eat, when you can earn your wages serving a wealthy monarch, and share in an empire that is not a mere hope but really exists?" He further made clear he had held off attacking thus far to spare *their* lives, not out of any concern for Demetrius. It was a pragmatic speech, an appeal to pragmatic men. Their loyalties lay with whoever could win, for winning meant plunder and power. They laid down their swords and spears and held up their hands in surrender, acclaiming Seleucus their leader and king from that moment.

Cut off with a few hundred men, Demetrius might have fought to the death like Leonidas at Thermopylae, but he chose self-preservation instead. With his last remaining supporters, he ran for the mountains. He still had his fleet as a fallback, though the nearest ships were at Caunus, six hundred miles to the west. Reaching them seemed like an impossible chance, but it was the only chance he had left. Concealed in a forest, he waited with his little band for nightfall, hoping to pick his way through the passes in darkness and take to the Caunus road.

An inventory was made of the food the men carried, with disastrous results. Their collective supplies would not last them even one day. Demetrius tried to think of a means of survival, when out of nowhere a ray of new hope burst forth. A man named Sosigenes, otherwise unknown, stepped forward and offered up a cache of gold coins he carried concealed in his belt. That money could buy them food, if they reached a place that had markets, and also hire them ships, or bribe the guards on the roads. Their situation suddenly seemed salvageable.

At nightfall Demetrius led the men forward, seeking the passes through the Amanus range. But Seleucus had anticipated this move and posted troops at the passes, instructing them to keep watch-fires burning all night. In the darkness Demetrius perceived that his routes were cut off. Though Seleucus might have let him slip quietly out of the region, back into lands that belonged to Lysimachus, it was clear now that Demetrius's former son-in-law meant to trap him, and do with him — what? The endgame was wholly unclear.

Demetrius brought his retinue back to the hiding place in the woods. The small group had shrunk even further, for more kept deserting, attracted like moths to the blazing fires in the passes. Those who remained were exhausted and losing their will to go on. A nameless soldier approached Demetrius and said what was on many minds: that he ought to stand down and give himself up to Seleucus.

At low ebbs before this, Demetrius had repeated the line from the Aeschylus play that spoke of a Fortune who always restored him, but he had never been at so low an ebb before. He was tired, having had no sleep the previous night, and his mountain retreat was cold and barren of food. In the depths of his anguish, death seemed preferable to surrender. Demetrius drew his sword and prepared to make an end of himself. But the men around him prevented him and tried to rally his spirits.

What hope could be offered now to a man who had none? Doubtless the Besieger's companions spoke of Stratonice, his daughter, future queen of the Seleucid realm as wife of Antiochus. Surely, they must have said, no ruler would mistreat the father of his son's bride, the grandfather of his own daughter.

Whatever they told him persuaded him to follow their counsel. He sent an envoy to Seleucus and offered to lay down his arms.

After perhaps an hour or two, a messenger from Seleucus arrived at the forest hideout. To the instant relief of Demetrius, this was a man he knew well: Apollonides, one of his own former officers. He brought the astonishing news that Seleucus regarded Demetrius as a friend and kinsman. A magnificent tent was being set up to receive the defeated king in royal style.

Fortune, it seemed, was once again kindling fires of hope. Demetrius would have an honored place at the side of Seleucus as a high-ranking adviser or, perhaps, a lieutenant commander. Word spread through the hills that Demetrius's star was again on the rise. Deserters and former friends made their way back to his side, racing to get there first. The Besieger's spirits revived as he saw his prospects brightening. Then a contingent of Seleucid troops arrived and surrounded the camp.

Plutarch explains what had happened, giving an account of Seleucus's change of heart remarkably similar to the earlier one — and similarly suspect. He describes Seleucus as delighted by the chance to show kindness to Demetrius, and sincere in his plans for a royal reception tent. But then, says Plutarch, malicious courtiers came forward. They noted the gathering strength of Demetrius's numbers and spoke of his dangerous hold on men's minds. As soon as Demetrius entered Seleucus's camp, they warned, he would draw defections and stir discontent. It was not safe to let such a man stay free.

The account reads like another product of the Seleucid spin factory. The truth was more likely this: Seleucus had once again put Demetrius off his guard with a soothing message, then closed his trap. Whatever his motives, he had added a last, and horribly cruel, twist to the downfall of the Antigonid house.

In the forest redoubt, a certain Pausanias, commander of the arrest squad, dismissed Demetrius's followers and took the Besieger away. He brought him to a fortress in Syria, inside a deep bend of the river Orontes and therefore nearly surrounded by water. This was to be his Elba, a place to contain a man of uncontainable ambition.

The great anabasis, Demetrius's quixotic adventure in Asia, had come to a close. It had cost thousands of lives and utterly destroyed the Besieger's reputation, which at the campaign's outset had still been potent enough to capture men's hopes. But those who had looked for a new crusade by a new Alexander had ended up bitterly disillusioned.

From his Syrian prison, Demetrius wrote to his son Antigonus and his captains, still holding on in Greece, and asked them to consider him dead and never obey any orders that came to them under his seal. He abdicated his kingship. Antigonus, Demetrius wrote, was now to be king in his place, and reign over whatever realm the family still held — and that wasn't much.

CHAPTER NINETEEN

The Final Crossing

The news of Demetrius's capture spread quickly through the Successor family—for by this time the Successors were one very big, very extended family. Ptolemy was father-in-law to Lysimachus and Demetrius, and stepfather-in-law to Pyrrhus, and all three of those men were fathers of Ptolemy's grandchildren. Demetrius had grandchildren by both Seleucus and Seleucus's son Antiochus; his son Alexander was Pyrrhus's nephew and was now living at Ptolemy's court. Ptolemy also had grandchildren by Lysimachus's son Agathocles, for he had married his daughters to the father and son. The interconnections of this sprawling clan surpass what genealogical charts can portray; a three-dimensional model might someday capture their complexity.

If ranked by number of intermarital credits, Demetrius came out on top of the hierarchy, Lysimachus on the bottom. Demetrius had linked his bloodlines not only to Ptolemy and Seleucus but also to Antipater (father of Cassander), a man whose fame and honor still glowed in European lands. That last link, by way of his marriage to Phila, had helped place Demetrius on the throne of Macedon, and it was currently helping his son Antigonus retain his position in Greece. Lysimachus, by contrast, had marital ties to Antipater's family as well, and several to Ptolemy's, but none at all to Demetrius or Seleucus, for both men despised him, as he despised them. That mutual hatred aligned Demetrius with Seleucus, as did the connection forged by Stratonice, by now the mother of a young boy, presumptive heir to the Seleucid realm.

The force of this alignment became clear in the wake of Demetrius's capture and imprisonment. Lysimachus, according to reports, sent an envoy to offer Seleucus a huge sum of money—two thousand talents of silver—to have Demetrius executed. Seleucus refused, and according to Plutarch felt disgust at the offer, which he considered loathsome and befitting a barbarian. To kill a rival in battle, as his own troops had killed Antigonus One-Eye at Ipsus, was one thing, but to snuff out the life of a captive, who could no longer do harm, was quite another. (It may be recalled that One-Eye himself, more than three decades before this, had snuffed out his own captive foe, the Greek captain Eumenes, in just this manner; but he had hesitated a long time before doing so. Demetrius, then only a teenager, had tried to dissuade his father from this murder.)

Other envoys kept arriving at Seleucus's court to plead not only for the life of Demetrius but for his release. The most earnest plea came from Antigonus Gonatas, Demetrius's devoted son, still in control of Piraeus and other Greek strongholds.

The young man had put on mourning garb when he heard of his father's capture, a stirring sight to those who admired filial devotion. Antigonus offered to surrender all his Greek territories to Seleucus as ransom, and even to come to Syria himself and take his father's place—thus, as hostage, ensuring that Demetrius would no longer do any harm. It is unclear why Seleucus refused such a generous offer. Rejected, Antigonus stayed where he was and carried on with the job his father assigned him in his dismal final epistle, maintaining a tiny remnant of a once-great empire.

What did Seleucus have in mind for his prisoner? According to two different sources — both perhaps influenced by court propaganda — Seleucus intended to free Demetrius and restore him to royal splendor, but wanted to give Antiochus the honor of clemency for the sake of the young man's queen, Stratonice.

Antiochus had been elevated by this time to the same royal rank as Seleucus, with rule over the eastern portion of Asia. He and Stratonice were living perhaps in Media, far from the Orontes River. Seleucus seems to have wanted them to come west to preside over Demetrius's liberation. For some unknown reason, they never did so — or perhaps the whole plan was a fiction intended to bolster Seleucus's image. The public must have wanted Demetrius freed; otherwise such a story, whatever its truth content, would never have circulated.

Demetrius remained in a kind of limbo, without a clear term of his sentence, both kinsman and foe to Seleucus. His quarters were set up to give him a royal lifestyle, complete with hunting, riding, sumptuous meals, and, no doubt, concubines to serve his sexual needs. Wine was allowed to flow freely at his table. Demetrius came to accept his new status, and did his best to stay active and keep in condition, so far as his small enclosure allowed. Little by little, his spirits began to revive.

Meanwhile, elsewhere in the ranks of the sprawling Successor family, troubles were brewing that for once had nothing to do with Demetrius — though they would have huge consequences for his son.

The polygamous ways of the Successors often created rival factions within their own houses, as sons from different wives competed for their father's throne. So it was in the house of Ptolemy. At the start of his reign over Egypt, Ptolemy had wed Eurydice, a high-ranking noblewoman, and she had borne him a son, whom he had named after himself. But then, in a rare case in which love won out over politics, Ptolemy shunted his wife aside and married one of her chambermaids, Berenice. With this woman too Ptolemy fathered a son, whom he *also* named after himself. Two junior Ptolemies were clearly destined to end up as rivals, especially given that the elder, who had received the nickname Ceraunus (Thunderbolt), could claim the throne based on order of birth, while the younger was sprung from a wife who was still her husband's queen.

As both boys reached their thirties and Ptolemy *père* his eighties, the issue of the succession became acute. Ceraunus must have sensed that he had the weaker position, for he left Egypt and took up residence with Lysimachus (as we have seen). His full sister, Lysandra, was married to Lysimachus's son Agathocles, so his branch of the Ptolemy clan—the children of Eurydice—had close links to that court. But so did the other branch, for Lysimachus himself was married to Arsinoe, Ptolemy's daughter by Berenice, his second wife and Agathocles' stepmother. The house of Lysimachus was thus split, in a rift parallel to the diverging halves of the house of Ptolemy.

At about the same time that Demetrius became a prisoner, Ptolemy made official what had already seemed inevitable, and named his younger namesake—his son by Berenice—his heir. In fact he promoted the man, today known as Ptolemy II or Ptolemy Philadelphus, to co-rulership of his realm, and father and son henceforth shared the title of king. Ceraunus, despite his primogeniture, was effectively dispossessed. In his exile in Thrace, he brooded over the preference shown by his father to his half-brother. Meanwhile the queen of that realm, Arsinoe, had seen her fortunes dramatically improve, now that her full brother was sharing the throne of Egypt.

Lysimachus was in a tight spot, as host to the cast-off son, but husband to the full sister of the new monarch. He had to choose sides, and, as any shrewd husband would do, he chose to support his wife's side of Ptolemy's family, in this case, Ptolemy II. His choice discomfited his son Agathocles, for *his* wife, Lysandra, belonged to the other side. New tensions arose between father and son in the house of Lysimachus.

Agathocles had always assumed he was heir to his father's throne, but now the succession was in some doubt. Lysimachus had three other sons, born to Arsinoe, and the eldest of these, *also named Ptolemy*, was now in his teens and eligible to hold power. This child was the full nephew of the reigning Egyptian king, so the prudent course for Lysimachus, as all could see, was to make *him* his heir. It was also clear to all that, should Agathocles manage to succeed his father, he would have to kill his half-brothers, whose claim to the throne would otherwise be supported by Egypt, perhaps by main force.

The rivalry for the succession became a duel to the death, pitting Arsinoe and Agathocles, stepmother and stepson, against each other. Which one acted first is unclear: either Agathocles began plotting to seize the throne with the help of Seleucus, or Arsinoe started a rumor that such a plot was in motion. Whatever the truth, Lysimachus grew convinced that Agathocles wanted him dead. He had his eldest son — the man who had won several battles for him, who had led the campaign that had rid him of Demetrius — killed. The watching world was repelled.

Agathocles' widow, Lysandra, fled to the court of Seleucus in Antiocheia, along with her brother Ceraunus. Disgusted by what he heard from them, and eager at last to take a hated foe down, Seleucus prepared for a showdown with Lysimachus. The weary world prepared for yet another Diadoch war, as the aging Successors continued to fight one another with the last of their strength.

Meanwhile, in his gilded imprisonment in Syria, Demetrius slowly gave up on his program of exercise, and no longer cared to go riding or hunting as he once had. Torpor overcame him, and he whiled away empty days in drinking and playing at dice. He put on weight, as his father had done, and his celebrated face grew fuller and rounder. He began to forget his dreams of global dominion, and the world outside began to forget about *him*.

Plutarch, who clearly admired the way Demetrius picked himself up every time he fell down, was fascinated by this final capitulation. He proposed two alternative explanations for the dramatic change. Demetrius may have been drowning his sorrows in drink, Plutarch surmises, or else he had taken to his new pursuits because "he realized that *this* was the way of life he had been longing for and pursuing from the start, though he had wandered off course through ignorance and false assumptions, giving much trouble to himself and to others as he sought for the Good in weapons and fleets and armies — the Good he now found where he did not expect it, in idleness, leisure, and rest."

Clearly Plutarch preferred this second theory, since it reinforced the point he went on to make: kings and commanders are foolish and bad, not only because they pursue pleasure and luxury instead of virtue, but because they cannot even enjoy what they've won when they've won it. He describes what we might now call the "type A personality," as seen in business tycoons who can never take a vacation. Plutarch chastises such men in *Demetrius,* yet in *Alexander,* another of his *Parallel Lives,* he crafted an admiring portrait of a king of the very same type. Much depended for Plutarch, it seems, on whether the ceaseless toil resulted in success or failure.

The gulf between the two ways of life Plutarch here contrasts — pursuit of power and rule or of pleasure and leisure — was vast, yet Demetrius had crossed it numerous times in his zigzag career, almost as often as he had crossed the Aegean. Plutarch considered Demetrius's nature to be that of a bifurcated obsessive. He threw himself into warfare with single-minded zeal but then, when the campaigning paused, indulged himself just as intensely in wine and in sex. He sported scandalously with Athenian courtesans one year, then sailed against Egypt the next with a fleet of unparalleled strength. Now that his campaigns were over for good, he fully committed himself to the banquet table, the game board, and, doubtless, the bed.

It was late in life to make such a dramatic turn. His body was used to the rigors of march and spare military rations, most of which were largely barley meal. He had also been ill several times in past years, perhaps with malaria; his most recent bout had laid him up for more than a month. The days of wine-soaked inactivity took their toll on his health. Within three years of his capture, having reached his mid-fifties, Demetrius was dead. He never escaped from his Elba to rally his forces again and make one more attempt at uniting the fragmented world.

Plutarch equivocates about the cause of death, saying both that Demetrius "grew ill," as though from disease, and that he was done in by surfeit of food and wine. Another source says simply that illness was the cause. Strangely, no one in ancient times suspected Seleucus of foul play, even though he had means, motive, and ample opportunity. Two modern scholars have suggested that Seleucus provided his prisoner with rich food and drink in the hope that these things would kill him; neither mentions the possibility of poison. The truth of such matters, of course, can never be known. The Seleucid propagandists no doubt made sure that the death was seen in the proper light by the public.

Indeed the public seems to have blamed Seleucus for not releasing his kinsman from prison in time to preserve his life. This at least is implied by Plutarch's account of Seleucus's bitter regret for his lack of clemency. Seleucus, Plutarch tells us, reproached himself with the thought that even a barbarous Thracian had released an imprisoned king, Lysimachus, and treated him with deference, while *he* had kept his own captive in shameful confinement. Such stories got about, in general, only because Seleucus wanted them to, so it seems that in this case he felt pressure to show contrition. Whatever his faults, whatever his failings, Demetrius had touched many hearts; his undignified death was felt to be morally wrong.

Seleucus had Demetrius cremated and placed his remains in a golden urn for shipment back to his son. This followed long-standing tradition among the Successors; the corpses of both Craterus and Eumenes had been honored in similar ways by the men who destroyed them. Antigonus Gonatas was in mainland Greece at the time of his father's cremation, but he launched his entire fleet — for he still had a large one — to meet the urn-bearing ship as it crossed the Aegean. Somewhere in the Cyclades, in a solemn encounter, Seleucus's men handed over the urn, and Antigonus took it aboard his flagship vessel, perhaps the giant sixteener his father had built but had never been able to use.

Antigonus had planned his father's last journey as a naval funeral procession, with stops at the ports of call where Antigonid power held sway. The urn, nestled within a purple robe and crowned with a diadem, was placed on the highest deck of the ship, where it could be seen by those standing on shore. A solemn honor guard of young men in arms was posted beside it.

At each stopping point, local dignitaries would come aboard the flagship and place garlands around the urn, in the way that flowers today are left at a grave. Some cities sent envoys dressed in funereal garb to join the procession and accompany the remains. The fleet stopped at numerous islands and doubtless put in at Piraeus (though Plutarch does not say so), for that busy hub was still in Antigonid hands, one of the key possessions the dynasty retained (and would retain for another half-century).

A final stop was at Corinth, another important Antigonid port and a city that, unlike most others, had never questioned its ties to Demetrius. Crowds of observers on shore beheld a moving spectacle, as the greatest musician of the day, Xenophantus, played a dirge on his *aulos,* a kind of double-chambered oboe, in time to the splashing strokes of the ship's many oars. Antigonus was seen on the deck of the ship, bowed over and in tears, as the music and oar strokes combined in a plangent rhythm, compared by Plutarch to a mourner beating his breast.

From there Antigonus sailed to the coast of Thessaly, where his father had built a city and named it after himself—Demetrias. The urn was interred there, no doubt in a splendid tomb, but the site has never been found.

Thus ended the life of Demetrius Poliorcetes.

At almost the same moment Antigonus was conducting the last rites for his father, Seleucus was preparing to march west into the lands that belonged to Lysimachus. Ostensibly he meant to avenge Agathocles, the son so callously murdered, but of course he had other goals to pursue, as did his new comrade-in-arms, the Thunderbolt, Ptolemy Ceraunus. This man had fled the court of Lysimachus with his sister Lysandra in the wake of the dynastic strife that erupted between the two daughters of Ptolemy, children of different mothers.

The forces of Seleucus and Lysimachus met at a place called Corrupedion. Little is known of what happened there, except that Seleucus won and Lysimachus, still leading troops in combat at roughly age eighty, was hit by a spear throw and killed. At last Seleucus had eliminated the man he most despised, and also gained full control of Anatolia.

Seleucus now saw hope of becoming what Demetrius had tried to be, the lord of both Europe and Asia. He crossed the Straits of Hellespont and planned to march onward to Macedon, to end his days as the king of his long-ago homeland. But as soon as he reached Thracian soil, Ceraunus, who saw his own chance for a throne, killed him with his own hands.

Demetrius had missed by only a year the chance to see two of his three great rivals, Lysimachus and Seleucus, die by violent means. Perhaps, though, he outlived the third, Ptolemy, who had slipped peacefully out of life the previous year — the only officer of Alexander the Great to die of natural causes.

Epilogue

Though he had failed in his efforts as king and army commander, failed even in his eponymous role of besieger, Demetrius did not fail in the ultimate goal of a dynast: to have his children inherit kingdoms and thrones.

Plutarch ends his *Demetrius* with a catalogue of the Besieger's children and the note that "his line continued to rule Macedon, descendant by descendant, down to Perseus, in whose time Macedon was conquered by the Romans." Antigonus, son of Demetrius and Phila, *did* claim that throne, after a force of invading Celts left it vacant by killing Ceraunus. Thereafter, five generations of Antigonids ruled in the land of Alexander the Great, spanning a century in which (as also noted by Plutarch) sons trusted fathers and fathers sons within the ruling family, and no one killed anyone else — a peace the Macedonian palace had rarely known.

Demetrius's son by Ptolemaïs also obtained a throne, in Cyrene, a Greek city on the North African coast. He too was named Demetrius and apparently had his father's good looks, for ancient historians know him as Demetrius the Beautiful.

But the greatest dynastic success of all came to Stratonice, Demetrius's daughter, who married first Seleucus and then Antiochus. Antiochus apparently took no other wives; he was content for a grandchild of Demetrius, whom he named Seleucus, to stand as his heir. Thus the Seleucid line can also be called the Demetrian line, and indeed the name Demetrius was borne by two of its subsequent rulers. It controlled the greatest of the Successor kingdoms, comprising a huge part of Asia, for two centuries, until it too was absorbed by imperial Rome.

At a certain point in the mid-third century BCE, there were children or grandchildren of the Besieger in power on all three continents. Thus, through his descendants, Demetrius succeeded, as much as anyone did, in uniting the former empire of Alexander the Great.

Chronology

All dates BCE. Dates 321–316 follow the so-called high chronology
and are one year earlier than those adopted by some other writers.

336	Birth of Demetrius in Macedon
333	Antigonus One-Eye appointed satrap of Phrygia
ca. 330	Demetrius arrives in Phrygia to join his father
323	Death of Alexander the Great; regency of Perdiccas and others
321	Departure of Demetrius and Antigonus from Asia
320	Triparadeisus conclave; marriage of Phila and Demetrius
ca. 319	Antigonus Gonatas born to Demetrius and Phila
317–316	Demetrius's first battles (leading cavalry against Eumenes)
312	Battle of Gaza (against Ptolemy)
311	Nabataean campaign; attack on Babylon to oust Seleucus
307	Demetrius's first invasion of Athens; ouster of Demetrius of Phalerum
306	Attack on Cyprus and naval defeat of Ptolemy; Lamia enters Demetrius's retinue; Demetrius and Antigonus assume the royal title and lead abortive invasion of Egypt
305	Start of the siege of Rhodes
304	Negotiated end to the siege of Rhodes; second Athens sojourn of Demetrius
303	Demetrius campaigns in the Peloponnese; marries Deidameia, sister of Pyrrhus
301	Battle of Ipsus; Death of Antigonus One-Eye; Athens banishes Demetrius
ca. 298	Marriage of Demetrius's daughter Stratonice to Seleucus; Demetrius retakes Cilicia
297	Death of Cassander and his son Philip; succession struggle in Macedon

Chronology

Genealogy

The family of Demetrius

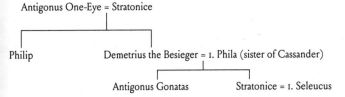

Antigonus One-Eye = Stratonice

Philip

Demetrius the Besieger = 1. Phila (sister of Cassander)

Antigonus Gonatas

Stratonice = 1. Seleucus

= 2. Antiochus, son of Seleucus

= 2. Eurydice (an Athenian)
|
Corrhabus

= 3. Deidameia (sister of Pyrrhus of Epirus)
|
Alexander

= 4. Lanassa (a Syracusan)

= 5. Ptolemaïs (daughter of Ptolemy)
|
Demetrius the Beautiful

(liaison with) Lamia (a hetaera)
|
Phila

Source Notes

The life of Demetrius is better known than those of any of his contemporaries, thanks largely to Plutarch's richly detailed *Demetrius,* one of the longest biographies contained in the *Parallel Lives.* I have relied substantially on that text and on the invaluable notes compiled by Thomas Rose for his doctoral dissertation (soon to be published in revised form), "A Historical Commentary on Plutarch's Life of Demetrius." All quotes from Plutarch and other Greek sources are given here in my own translation. Plutarch's *Pyrrhus* and *Eumenes,* both found in the *Parallel Lives,* overlap with the events of Demetrius's life even while focusing on other figures.

Diodorus Siculus's *Library of History* is the other major source for what is known of Demetrius and his times. Unfortunately the work is incomplete for about half of the period in which Demetrius lived. Diodorus's twentieth book, nearly intact, takes us up to the preparations for the Battle of Ipsus, but the twenty-first book is preserved only in sparse fragments that give few glimpses of Demetrius during the next two decades. The loss is grave, because here and in the previous book Diodorus relied on Hieronymus of Cardia, a talented historian and an eyewitness to many of the events described there.

Even more fragmentary than Diodorus's account of this era is the *Philippica* of Pompeius Trogus, a once-voluminous history of the Macedonian empire, now almost totally lost but known through a bare-bones summary made much later by the Roman writer Justin. Books 13 through 16 of Justin's *Epitome,* as it is known, preserve a skeletal version of the original narrative of Pompeius Trogus, frustratingly thin but nevertheless a source of some unique and valuable information (though sometimes at odds with other sources).

A few anecdotes and stories concerning Demetrius can be recovered from Plutarch's moral treatises as well as from a work nearly contemporary with Plutarch, Athenaeus's *Deipnosophistae,* a collection of table talk miscellanea. Other scattered bits of information emerge from the works of Strabo, Appian, Pausanias, and Cornelius Nepos. Book 4 of the *Stratagems* of Polyaenus preserves twelve military ruses ascribed to Demetrius and twenty more to his father, for both men were renowned in antiquity as tricksters and strategists.

Among the secondary works I have relied on, special mention must be made of the recent, very thorough *Demetrius the Besieger* by Wheatley and Dunn; the much older but magisterial work of Tarn, *Antigonus Gonatas,* a biography of Demetrius's eldest son that also deals in depth with the career of the man himself; and Billows, *Antigonos the One-Eyed and the Creation of the Hellenistic State.* One or another of these three

Source Notes

works helped illuminate nearly every aspect of Demetrius's career, often with intriguing differences of perspective (Wheatley and Dunn, for example, are much kinder to Demetrius than Billows). Other partial or full biographies of Demetrius include Wehrli, *Antigone et Démétrios,* and Manni, *Demetrio Poliorcete.*

The following general studies of Demetrius's era have also been consulted throughout (more specific sources are mentioned below in the notes): Anson, *Alexander's Heirs;* Green, *Alexander to Actium;* Hammond and Griffith, *History of Macedonia;* Heckel, *Who's Who in the Age of Alexander the Great;* Macurdy, *Hellenistic Queens;* Ogden, *Polygamy, Prostitutes and Death;* Roisman, *Alexander's Veterans;* and Will, "Adventures of Demetrius Poliorcetes."

CHAPTER 1. HIS FATHER'S SON

The events of this chapter — attested by Plutarch, Diodorus, Arrian, and others — are closely examined in my *Ghost on the Throne,* as well as in the early chapters of Waterfield's *Dividing the Spoils* and the later ones of Anson's *Eumenes of Cardia.* Plutarch reports the rumor that Demetrius was actually the nephew of Antigonus in chapter 2 of *Demetrius* (*Demetrius* 2); evidently it was based on the fact that Antigonus had married his brother's widow not long before his eldest son's birth (which means he was functionally, even if not biologically, the boy's father). The relationship between Demetrius and Antigonus is explored from different perspectives by Wheatley and Dunn (*Demetrius the Besieger,* pp. 9–11, 49–51) and Billows (*Antigonos the One-Eyed and the Creation of the Hellenistic State,* pp. 9–10, 139–140); both agree with Plutarch that it was warm and affectionate. The story concerning the young man's resistance to marriage comes from Plutarch, *Demetrius* 14, and his sexual activities in youth are described in chapter 19. The question of royal Macedonian polygamy and how it became more widespread is taken up in Ogden, *Polygamy, Prostitutes and Death.*

CHAPTER 2. THE APPRENTICESHIP OF A GENERAL

Diodorus's words about the intelligence of Eumenes and Antigonus come from book 19 of *Library of History,* chapter 26. The anecdote in which Antigonus upbraids his son for asking about their departure time comes from Plutarch, *Demetrius* 28; Plutarch does not give it a datable context but says only that Demetrius was then still a *meirakion,* a "lad," a term that might conceivably fit his age at the time of the Media march, eighteen or nineteen. The battles in which Demetrius charged the forces of Eumenes, Paraetacene and Gabene, are discussed by Anson (*Eumenes of Cardia,* pp. 176–188), and a battle map of Gabene (there spelled Gabiene) is supplied by Wheatley and Dunn (*Demetrius the Besieger,* p. 44). The shifting loyalties of the Silver Shields, and other Alexander veterans, are chronicled by Joseph Roisman in *Alexander's Veterans.*

Source Notes

CHAPTER 3. THE DUEL WITH PTOLEMY (I)

The rise of Seleucus is chronicled by Grainger (*Seleukos Nikator*), and the early support offered him by Ptolemy (and the other foes of Antigonus) is discussed by Worthington (*Ptolemy I*, pp. 116–118). The dream of Antigonus regarding Mithridates is related by both Plutarch (*Demetrius* 4) and Appian (*Mithridatic* Wars chapter 9). Demetrius's speech to his men before the Battle of Gaza is in Diodorus (*Library of History* 19.81). Wheatley and Dunn give an extensive account of the battle in *Demetrius the Besieger* (pp. 63–72), complete with a battle map. Ptolemy's message to Demetrius, accompanying the return of his officers, is difficult to interpret, as Thomas Rose has acknowledged to me in a private exchange; the paraphrase offered here is my own.

CHAPTER 4. PETRA AND BABYLON

Hieronymus of Cardia, one of the most lamented lost authors of Greek antiquity, is the subject of an eponymous book by Jane Hornblower. Demetrius's Nabataean campaign (in which Hieronymus likely participated) is examined there (pp. 144 ff.), as well as in Bosworth, *The Legacy of Alexander* (pp. 188–209). The identification of the site of Demetrius's siege as Petra is not certain, and Bosworth (pp. 202–203) proposes a different rock citadel some thirty miles north of Petra. Demetrius's Babylon campaign is discussed in depth by Wheatley and Dunn (*Demetrius the Besieger*, chapter 7), who bring to bear evidence from the Babylonian Chronicles, a set of terse cuneiform records of political and military events.

CHAPTER 5. ATHENS AND MEGARA

The Antigonid policy of "freedom for the Greeks" is dealt with in detail by Billows (*Antigonos the One-Eyed*, chapter 6), who regards it as something more substantial than a cynical propaganda ploy. For Demetrius's complex relations with Athens beginning in 307 and extending for the next two decades, see the third chapter of Habicht, *Athens from Alexander to Antony*. The Cratesipolis episode cannot be placed securely in either time or space; the emendation of Plutarch's text in *Demetrius* 9 in order to place the rendezvous at Pagae rather than Patrae (first proposed by Johann Kaltwasser in the early nineteenth century) makes Plutarch's chronology possible, but both the emendation and the chronology may be wrong. Wheatley and Dunn prefer to place the episode in the context of Demetrius's 303 Peloponnesian campaign (*Demetrius the Besieger*, p. 123). Plutarch's chronology of the honors awarded to Demetrius by Athens (*Demetrius* 10–12) is also vague and confused, with three different layers of honors flattened into one; I have followed the time lines established by Wheatley and Dunn (pp. 128–138) and Rose, "A Historical Commentary on Plutarch's Life of Demetrius."

Source Notes

CHAPTER 6. THE DUEL WITH PTOLEMY (II)

Wheatley and Dunn supply a useful map of the Cyprus campaign (*Demetrius the Besieger*, p. 152), which is also described in detail by Diodorus (*Library of History* 20.47–53). Worthington reprints a reconstruction of the helepolis made by Evan Mason (*Ptolemy I*, p. 159). The elevation of Antigonus and Demetrius to kingship is explored in the important article by Erich Gruen, "The Coronation of the Diadochi." Plutarch describes the Antigoneia episode in *Demetrius* 17–18; nearly all recent writers on the episode regard it as a piece of political theater arranged in advance by Antigonus.

CHAPTER 7. THE DUEL WITH PTOLEMY (III)

William Murray's *The Age of Titans* does a very good survey of shipbuilding advances and (mostly) enlargements in the age of the Successors, often with specific reference to Demetrius. Experts diverge as to what went wrong for the Antigonids on the Egyptian campaign; Billows speaks of "the failure of the fleet to turn Ptolemy's defensive position" (*Antigonos the One-Eyed*, p. 164) whereas Wheatley and Dunn stress the effect of the late-season departure (Antigonus's choice) and ask, "Why . . . did he [Antigonus] not attempt an opportunistic crossing [of the Nile] while Ptolemy was facing Demetrius at the Phatnitic mouth? . . . It seems quite incredible that no assault at all was attempted" (*Demetrius the Besieger*, pp. 175–176).

CHAPTER 8. ASSAULT ON RHODES (I)

The squeeze in which Rhodes found itself in the late fourth century and the resulting siege it suffered are dealt with in Richard M. Berthold's *Rhodes in the Hellenistic Age*. The detailed account of the siege by Diodorus Siculus (*Library of History* 20.82 ff.) indicates that he used not only Hieronymus of Cardia as a source but a Rhodian writer as well, someone who was an eyewitness to events inside the walls. Plutarch by contrast gives a very sketchy account of the siege in *Demetrius* 21–23. Wheatley and Dunn as usual supply an illustrative map (*Demetrius the Besieger*, p. 189). The Rhodian inscription recording the instructions from Athena is known as the Lindos Chronicle; the last of its surviving miracle stories relates the dream of Callicles. For the importance of elephants in Seleucus's army, see Bar-Kochva, *The Seleucid Army* (pp. 75 ff.). Plutarch's words about Demetrius's love of gigantism come from chapter 20 of *Demetrius*.

CHAPTER 9. ASSAULT ON RHODES (II)

My estimate of the size of the Rhodes helepolis comes from Marsden, *Greek and Roman Artillery* (p. 84). Wheatley and Dunn (*Demetrius the Besieger*) speculate that the manpower drain created by the helepolis depleted Demetrius's navy and made possible the extremely damaging Rhodian sorties of the winter of 304–303. The tale of the preservation of Protogenes' painting is variously told by Plutarch (*Demetrius* 22), Aulus Gellius (*Attic Nights* 15.31), and Pliny the Elder (*Natural History* 35.36.104–106). In a particularly pro-Demetrian version of the story, the siege of Rhodes was broken off in order to spare the painting. Historians disagree on the extent to which the siege was a failure for the Antigonids, with some seeing an on-balance win in the family's demonstration of its power. The idea that the sale of the helepolis parts enabled Rhodes to build the Colossus derives from Pliny the Elder; Wheatley and Dunn (*Demetrius the Besieger*, pp. 444–446) decline to comment on its veracity. Diodorus notes the effect of the Rhodians' honoring their alliance and describes the workings of the battering rams at *Library of History* 20.93.

CHAPTER 10. DEMETRIUS THE DESCENDER

See the notes to Chapter 5, above, on the difficulties of sorting out the different chronological layers in the honors awarded by Athens to Demetrius. The weaving of his and his father's image may have taken place during his sojourn in Athens in 307, as Diodorus indicates (*Library of History* 20.46), in which case it may have been rent by the wind during the Panathenaia of 306, not 302. The degree to which Demetrius deliberately assimilated himself to Dionysus is unclear, in part because the horns on his coin profile could evoke either that god or Pan. The fictional letter from Lamia to Demetrius is the first in Book 2 of Alciphron's *Letters of the Courtesans*, available with translation and notes in P. Granholm's edition of that work (Uppsala: University of Uppsala Press, 2012). Demetrius's ability to draw rubberneckers with his beauty is attested by Plutarch (*Demetrius* 2), which also has the quote from Philippides.

CHAPTER 11. THE WAR OF THE FIVE ARMIES

Demetrius's lack of resolution of the campaign against Cassander has been variously interpreted; Billows calls it a "culpable lack of energy on the part of Demetrius" (*Antigonos the One-Eyed,* p. 175), while Wheatley and Dunn see the Besieger poised to strike a fatal blow at just the moment the summons from Antigonus arrives: "Demetrius was prevented from concluding a campaign by his father's peremptory directives" (*Demetrius the Besieger,* p. 235). The story of Demetrius's warm kisses when greeting his father is found in Plutarch, *Demetrius* 19; in chapter 28 Plutarch describes Antigonus presenting Demetrius to the army as the "successor" to his realm. Lysimachus's destruction of the Autiaratae troops in his army is described by Polyaenus (*Stratagems* 4.12.1), with very vague context; some scholars (e.g., Bosworth, *Legacy of Alexander,* p. 248), believe it belongs to a later campaign than that of the Battle of Ipsus, but both Billows (p. 180) and Wheatley and Dunn (p. 245) place it in 301. The latter authors supply a useful pair of maps (p. 248) to illustrate the course of the battle itself. Demetrius's dream about Alexander before the Battle of Ipsus and the course of the battle are in Plutarch, *Demetrius* 29.

Source Notes

CHAPTER 12. LORD OF THE ISLES

For Demetrius's various coin issues and their iconography, see Newell's survey *The Coinage of Demetrius Poliorcetes,* and the extensive discussion by Wheatley and Dunn of the post-Ipsus issues (*Demetrius the Besieger,* pp. 263–277). On Pyrrhus see Garoufalias, *Pyrrhus: King of Epirus;* there is as yet no scholarly commentary on Plutarch's life. It is unclear why the marriage between Demetrius and Ptolemy's daughter was postponed for so long; Ogden (*Polygamy, Prostitutes and Death*) only cites the unconvincing theory of Macurdy (*Hellenistic Queens,* pp. 64–68) that Demetrius wanted to avoid antagonizing Phila. On Seleucus considering his territory "enough for more heirs than one" see Plutarch, *Demetrius* 31.

CHAPTER 13. IN SEARCH OF A KINGDOM

On the tyranny of Lachares and Demetrius's intervention in Athens to end it, see Ferguson, "Lachares and Demetrius Poliorcetes," and Habicht, *Athens from Alexander to Antony.* The speech by which Demetrius won the support of the Macedonian army is preserved (in some version) by Justin (*Epitome* 16.1.9), with partial confirmation (of the context at least) by Plutarch in his description of Alexander's death (*Demetrius* 37). Wheatley and Dunn are fairly certain that Demetrius contrived the fiction that he had killed Alexander in self-defense (*Demetrius the Besieger,* p. 327).

CHAPTER 14. "THEN DON'T BE A KING"

The sequence of Demetrius's marriages and offspring can best be followed with the help of Ogden, *Polygamy, Prostitutes and Death* (pp. 173–178). On the transfer of Stratonice from Seleucus to his son, and the legends explaining it, see chapter 5 of Ogden's *The Legend of Seleucus.* The exchange between the angry petitioner and Demetrius is given in Plutarch, *Demetrius* 42. The hymn that greeted the entry of Demetrius and Lanassa into Athens, hailing them as gods, is preserved in Athenaeus (*Deipnosophistae* 253b–f); it is discussed by Wheatley and Dunn (*Demetrius the Besieger,* chapter 22). Plutarch oddly omits the hymn from his life of Demetrius, though he records many other divine honors awarded by Athens. Plutarch describes Demetrius as quoting Aeschylus in *Demetrius* 35. Vitruvius's anecdote about the use of sewage against the helepolis is found at *On Architecture* 10.16.4–7; the suggestion that this may have been done by the Thebans was made by Campbell (*Besieged,* p. 87).

CHAPTER 15. THE UNRAVELING

There is evidence that Demetrius was levying heavy taxes on his Macedonian and Greek subjects to finance the invasion of Asia; Diogenes Laertius reports that Eretria employed a philosopher, Menedemus, to plead with Demetrius for a reduction (*Lives of the Eminent Philosophers* 2.17.140). No doubt this damaged his popularity and contributed to the desertions drawn by Lysimachus and Pyrrhus. The suicide of Phila is recounted by Plutarch (*Demetrius* 45) in a single vague sentence; we do not know whether Demetrius was with her at the time. Wheatley and Dunn astutely suggest that she may have killed herself directly after hearing of her husband's defeat, on the assumption that he would not be able to get her safely out of Cassandreia (*Demetrius the Besieger,* p. 389). Plutarch discusses Demetrius's dress and theatrical tendencies in chapter 41 of *Demetrius.* Pyrrhus's report of his dream is related by Plutarch in *Pyrrhus* 11. The comedy of Philippides quoted by Plutarch is found in two segments (reassembled here), in chapters 12 and 26 of *Demetrius.*

CHAPTER 16. A KING IN PLAIN CLOTHES

The revolt of the Athenians after Demetrius's overthrow in Macedon is understood largely from the so-called Callias decree, a stone inscription honoring a benefactor of Athens; it is discussed in depth in Shear, *Kallias of Sphettos and the Revolt of Athens in 286 B.C.* A second, less revealing inscription concerning Callias's brother Phaedrus, is discussed by Wheatley and Dunn (*Demetrius the Besieger,* p. 399).

CHAPTER 17. THE GREAT ANABASIS

Wheatley and Dunn (*Demetrius the Besieger,* p. 408) supply a useful map of Demetrius's movements in 286–285 as he advanced into Asia and withdrew from the coast while Agathocles chased him eastward. The details of the anabasis and the capture and death of Demetrius are taken from the account of Plutarch (*Demetrius* 46–52); they derive from a participant, perhaps Hieronymus of Cardia (Wheatley and Dunn, p. 420). Plutarch's account of the Lycus crossing is contradicted by Polyaenus (*Stratagems* 4.7.12); there seems little hope of reconciling the two or determining which is more accurate. The quote giving Plutarch's assessment of Pyrrhus's need to keep his soldiers busy comes from chapter 11 of *Pyrrhus.* The story of the Phrygian farmer digging to find Antigonus comes from chapter 29 of Plutarch's *Phocion.* The story of how Lysimachus used a pirate as an agent to regain Ephesus is in Polyaenus (*Stratagems* 5.19).

CHAPTER 18. TWISTS OF THE KNIFE

The tombs of the 420 Athenians slaughtered in the attempt to take the Hill of the Muses were honored with a monument at Athens (Pausanias, *Description of Greece* 1.29.10). Polyaenus's collection of the stratagems of Seleucus confirms at several points the detailed account given by Plutarch (*Demetrius* 46). At *Stratagems* 4.9.5 Polyaenus records that Seleucus had watchfires lit in mountain passes to deter Demetrius from attempting to escape. At 4.9.2–3 Polyaenus supports Plutarch's account of the two last desperate efforts Demetrius made against Seleucus and even echoes closely Justin's version of the speech Seleucus made to turn Demetrius's men against him. Plutarch describes Demetrius as being "like a wild beast" at *Demetrius* 48; chapters 48–51 describe Demetrius's last battles and capture.

CHAPTER 19. THE FINAL CROSSING

For the machinations at the court of Lysimachus, see Elizabeth Carney's *Arsinoe II of Egypt and Macedon* (Oxford: Oxford University Press, 2013), and the last chapter of Helen Lund's *Lysimachus: A Study in Early Hellenistic Kingship* (London: Routledge, 1992). Peter Green suggested that Seleucus gave Demetrius rich food and wine to hasten his death (*Alexander to Actium*, p. 130). Plutarch's speculation about the causes of Demetrius's decline come in chapter 52 of *Demetrius;* the details of the funeral rites are supplied in the subsequent chapter.

EPILOGUE

The career of Demetrius's son and the ultimate success of the Antigonid dynasty can now be followed with the help of Waterfield, *The Making of a King*, in addition to Tarn's richly detailed, but dated, 1913 study, *Antigonus Gonatas*.

Bibliography

ANCIENT SOURCES

Appian, *The Mithridatic Wars*. Trans. Horace White. Livius. https://www.livius.org
/sources/content/appian/appian-the-mithridatic-wars.

Athenaeus. *Deipnosophistae* (*The Learned Banqueters*). Trans. S. Douglas Olson. Loeb
Classical Library 204. Cambridge: Harvard University Press, 2007.

Aulus Gellius. *Attic Nights*. 3 vols. Vol. 3: *Books 14–20*. Trans. J. C. Rolfe. Loeb Classical Library 212. Cambridge: Harvard University Press, 1927.

Cornelius Nepos. *On Greet Generals*. Trans. J. C. Rolfe. Loeb Classical Library 467.
Cambridge: Harvard University Press, 1929.

Diodorus Siculus. *The Library* [*Library of History*]. Vol. 2: *Books 16–20: Philip II, Alexander the Great, and the Successors*. Trans. Robin Waterfield. Oxford World Classics. Oxford: Oxford University Press, 2019.

Diogenes Laertius. *Lives of the Eminent Philosophers*. Trans. Pamela Mensch. Ed. James
Miller. New York: Oxford University Press, 2018.

Justin. *Epitome of the "Philippic History" of Pompeius Trogus*. 2 vols. Vol. 2: *Books 13–15:
The Successors to Alexander the Great*. Trans. J. C. Yardley. Clarendon Ancient History Series. Oxford: Oxford University Press, 2011.

Pausanias. *Description of Greece*. 5 vols. Vol. 1: *Books 1–2: Attica and Corinth*. Trans.
W. H. S. Jones. Loeb Classical Library 93. Cambridge: Harvard University Press,
1918.

Pliny the Elder. *Natural History*. 10 vols. Vol. 9: *Books 33–35*. Trans. H. Rackham. Loeb
Classical Library 394. Cambridge: Harvard University Press, 1952.

Plutarch. *Parallel Lives*. In Plutarch, *The Age of Alexander: Ten Greek Lives*. Rev. ed. Trans.
Ian Scott Kilvert and Timothy E. Duff. Penguin Classics. London: Penguin, 2011.

Polyaenus. *Stratagems*. Rev. ed. Trans. R. Shepherd. Attalus. http://www.attalus.org
/info/polyaenus.html.

Strabo. *Geography*. 8 vols. Vol. 4: *Books 8–9*. Trans. Horace Leonard Jones. Loeb Classical Library 196. Cambridge: Harvard University Press, 1927.

Vitruvius. *On Architecture*. 2 vols. Vol. 2: *Books 6–10*. Trans. Frank Granger. Loeb Classical Library 280. Cambridge: Harvard University Press, 1934.

Bibliography

MODERN SOURCES

Anson, Edward. *Alexander's Heirs: The Age of the Successors.* Malden, Mass.: Blackwell, 2014.

Anson, Edward. *Eumenes of Cardia: A Greek Among the Macedonians.* Leiden: Brill, 2004.

Bar-Kochva, B. *The Seleucid Army.* Cambridge: Cambridge University Press, 1976.

Berthold, Richard M. *Rhodes in the Hellenistic Age.* Ithaca: Cornell University Press, 1984.

Billows, Richard. *Antigonos the One-Eyed and the Creation of the Hellenistic State.* Berkeley: University of California Press, 1990.

Bosworth, A. B. *The Legacy of Alexander: Politics, Warfare, and Propaganda Under the Successors.* Oxford: Oxford University Press, 2002.

Campbell, Duncan B. *Besieged: Siege Warfare in the Ancient World.* Oxford: Osprey, 2006.

Ferguson, W. S. "Lachares and Demetrius Poliorcetes." *Classical Philology* 24 (1929): 1–31.

Garoufalias, Petros. *Pyrrhus: King of Epirus.* London: Stacey International, 1979.

Grainger, J. *Seleukos Nikator: Constructing a Hellenistic Kingdom.* London: Routledge, 1990.

Green, Peter. *Alexander to Actium: The Historical Evolution of the Hellenistic Age.* Berkeley: University of California Press, 1990.

Gruen, Erich. "The Coronation of the Diadochi." In *The Craft of the Ancient Historian,* ed. J. Eadie and J. Ober, 253–271. Lanham, Md.: Rowman and Littlefield, 1985.

Habicht, Christian. *Athens from Alexander to Antony.* Cambridge: Harvard University Press, 1997.

Hammond, N. G. L., and G. T. Griffith. *A History of Macedonia, 336–167 B.C.* Oxford: Oxford University Press, 1988.

Heckel, Waldemar. *Who's Who in the Age of Alexander the Great.* Oxford: Oxford University Press, 2006.

Hornblower, Jane. *Hieronymus of Cardia.* New York: Oxford University Press, 1982.

Lund, Helen. *Lysimachus: A Study in Early Hellenistic Kingship.* London: Routledge, 1992.

Macurdy, G. H. *Hellenistic Queens: A Study of Woman-Power in Macedonia, Seleucid Syria, and Ptolemaic Egypt.* Baltimore: Johns Hopkins University Press, 1932.

Bibliography

Manni, Eugenio. *Demetrio Poliorcete.* Rome: Signorelli, 1951.

Marsden, E. W. *Greek and Roman Artillery: Historical Development.* Oxford: Oxford University Press, 1969.

Murray, William. *The Age of Titans: The Rise and Fall of the Great Hellenistic Navies.* Oxford: Oxford University Press, 2014.

Newell, Edward. *The Coinage of Demetrius Poliorcetes.* Oxford: Oxford University Press, 1927.

Ogden, Daniel. *The Legend of Seleucus: Kingship, Narrative and Mythmaking in the Ancient World.* Cambridge: Cambridge University Press, 2017.

Ogden, Daniel. *Polygamy, Prostitutes and Death: The Hellenistic Dynasties.* London: Duckworth, 1999.

Roisman, J. *Alexander's Veterans and the Early Wars of the Successors.* Austin: University of Texas Press, 2012.

Romm, James. *Ghost on the Throne: The Death of Alexander the Great and the War for Crown and Empire.* New York: Knopf, 2011.

Rose, Thomas. "A Historical Commentary on Plutarch's Life of Demetrius." Ph.D. Diss. University of Iowa, 2015.

Shear, T. Leslie, Jr. *Kallias of Sphettos and the Revolt of Athens in 286 B.C.* Princeton: Princeton University Press, 1978.

Tarn, William. *Antigonus Gonatas.* Oxford: Oxford University Press, 1913.

Waterfield, Robin. *Dividing the Spoils: The War for Alexander the Great's Empire.* Oxford: Oxford University Press, 2011.

Waterfield, Robin. *The Making of a King: Antigonus Gonatas of Macedon and the Greeks.* Chicago: University of Chicago Press, 2021.

Wehrli, Claude. *Antigone et Démétrios.* Geneva: Librairie Droz, 1968.

Wheatley, Pat, and Charlotte Dunn. *Demetrius the Besieger.* Oxford: Oxford University Press, 2020.

Will, É. "The Adventures of Demetrius Poliorcetes." In *The Cambridge Ancient History,* ed. F. W. Walbank et al. Vol. 7, pt. 1, pp. 101–109. Cambridge: Cambridge University Press, 1984.

Worthington, Ian. *Ptolemy I: King and Pharaoh of Egypt.* Oxford: Oxford University Press, 2016.

Index

Index

Antigonus I One-Eye (father of Demetrius): under Alexander in Asia, 4–5; alliance of Ptolemy, Lysimachus, and Cassander against, 21, 23–25; Asia, control of, 34; assassination of Cleopatra (sister of Alexander), 42; attempting to invade Egypt, 63–68; capture of treasury of Susa, 20, 24; crusade against Eumenes, 11–12, 15–21, 174; death of, at Battle of Ipsus, 114, 115, 174; deification of, by Athenians, 51–52, 89; and Demetrius's takeover of Macedonia, 131; distrust of officer class, 24, 25–26; king, taking title of, 60–61, 88; loss of eye in battle, 1; memory of, in Asia, 157; Peace of the Dynasts, 40–41; Perdiccas's dislike of, 6; receiving news of capture of Cyprus, 59–60; relationship with Demetrius, 17, 26–27; Rhodes, alliance with, 55; Rhodes, siege of, 69–70, 77, 86; rumors about relationship to Demetrius, 6. *See also* War of the Five Armies; Wars of the Successors

Antigonus Gonatas (son of Demetrius), 13–14, 77, 134, 136–137, 140, 144, 145, 153–154, 165–166, 172, 174–175, 180, 181, 183

Antiocheia, 119

Antiochus (son of Seleucus), 112–113, 118, 135, 153, 160, 170–171, 173, 175, 184

Antipater (father of Cassander), 3, 6–7, 9–12, 15–16, 21, 33, 89, 139, 173, 174

Antipater (son of Cassander), 129, 131

Antony, Mark, 49, 96

Apama, 118

Aphrodite (deity), 97, 127, 139

Apollonides, 171

Arabs, 36–41, 65, 162

Aristodemus, 47, 59–60

Aristotle, 49

Arsinoe (daughter of Ptolemy I), 118, 176–177, 182

Artemis, Temple of (Ephesus), 115–116

asphalt deposits, Dead Sea, 39

Athena (deity), 71, 92–93, 100, 111, 126, 153

Athenaeus (Antigonid officer), 36–38

Athenaeus (author), 127

Athenagoras, 82

Athens: Acropolis, 46, 92, 100, 153; banishment of Demetrius after Battle of Ipsus, 115, 116–117; at Battle of Salamis, 59; captured by Demetrius, 45–53, 56; Cassander and, 36–37, 76, 86, 89, 91–92, 98–99; concerns over autocracy and libertinage of Demetrius, 93–98; deification of Antigonus in, 51–52, 89; deification of consorts of Demetrius in, 127, 139; deification of Demetrius in, 51–52, 89, 90–93, 100–101, 127–128, 138–139; Dionysian cult, Demetrius linking himself to, 91–92, 100, 126; Eleusinian mysteries, induction of Demetrius into, 99–100; Hill of the Muses, garrison force on, 127, 149, 151, 166; initial establishment of Demetrius in, 89–101; liberation of Greek city-states promised by Antigonids, 40, 45, 88, 90, 93; lost to Demetrius after fall of Macedonia, 149–154, 165–166; Munychia fortress, 47, 48, 50, 51, 165–166; Panathenaia in, 92, 100; Parthenon, 92–93, 94, 126, 151; petitions, failures of Demetrius to hear, 140; political instability in, 89–90; retaken by Demetrius,

Index

Index

Index

Index

Index

Index